19th-Century Fiction and Non-fiction

Edited by Christopher Edge

OXFORD
UNIVERSITY PRESS

Great Clarendon Street, Oxford, OX2 6DP,
United Kingdom

Oxford University Press is a department of the University of Oxford.
It furthers the University's objective of excellence in research, scholarship,
and education by publishing worldwide. Oxford is a registered trade mark
of Oxford University Press in the UK and in certain other countries

British Library Cataloguing in Publication Data

Data available

ISBN 978-0-19-835740-7

3 5 7 9 10 8 6 4

Printed in China by Printplus Ltd

Acknowledgements

Extracts from H G Wells : *The Wheels of Chance* (first published by Dent,
1895) and *The Invisible Man* (first published in *Pearson's Weekly*, 1897, and
by Thomas Nelson & Sons, 1910), are reprinted by permission of United
Agents LLC on behalf of the Literary Executors of the Estate of H G Wells.

Cover image © amana images inc./Alamy

Contents

Introduction

What comes into your mind when you think about the 19th century? Foggy gas-lit streets and the rattle of a horse-drawn carriage? A dashing explorer slashing his way through dense jungle in search of lost treasure? Ladies in bonnets or the deerstalker of Sherlock Holmes? The 19th century was an era where great advances in science rubbed shoulders with a stubborn belief in the supernatural; an age of adventure but also a time of the most hideous of crimes.

In this collection you will read fiction, non-fiction and literary non-fiction from every decade of the 19th century, organised into themes that help you to explore different aspects of life at this time. There are extracts from novels and short stories as well as an array of non-fiction and literary non-fiction sources.

The extracts in this collection have been arranged so that the different texts help to illuminate each other, helping you to draw connections between non-fiction and fiction and build a picture of the time in which these texts were first written and read. For example, you will read eyewitness accounts of a scientific experiment from 1803, then read an extract from Mary Shelley's introduction to her novel *Frankenstein* where she explains how similar experiments inspired this story, before reading an extract from the novel itself which describes Victor Frankenstein's own experiment.

The 19th century was a time of great change but in many ways it also saw the birth of the modern age. As you read the extracts in this collection, I hope you will see reflections of the lives we live today, from fascination with the latest technological gadgets to worries about crime and poverty. In his 19th-century novel *Lord Jim*, the author Joseph Conrad wrote:

"My task, which I am trying to achieve is, by the power of the written word, to make you hear, to make you feel – it is, before all, to make you see. That – and no more – and it is everything."

I hope the power of the words in this collection achieve the same.

Christopher Edge

School and childhood

At the start of the 19th century, life for most children was very different from the lives of children today. Education was for the rich with wealthy families sending their sons to fee-paying schools, whilst their daughters were taught at home by governesses. Poorer children were expected to work to support their families and their only chance of education came from schools set up by charities. It was only in the late 19th century that the British Parliament passed laws to make it compulsory for every child between the ages of five and ten to attend school.

However in many other ways a Victorian childhood wasn't very different from the experiences of children today. You could see busy playgrounds filled with children playing, although the toys and games played might not be the same as those played today. Bullying could be found in the school playground, whilst friends might fall out and even find themselves in a fight.

A Letter about Ragged Schools

Ragged schools were schools set up to provide a free education for poor and deprived children in towns and cities. They relied on charitable donations and the following extract is taken from a fundraising pamphlet entitled *A Letter about Ragged Schools*, which was published in 1853.

There are hundreds of poor children who have either no home to go to, or such an one as you would fear to enter; that many pass the night under arches, or on the steps of doors, or wherever they can – poor unhappy little beings! Oh! when you pray for yourselves, and ask God to bless your father and mother, your brothers and sisters, then do not forget to ask Him also to help the poor outcasts.

Now, Ragged Schools have been set on foot by kind and Christian people on purpose to do good to these unhappy children. They are brought to these schools, and there they have their torn, dirty clothes taken off, and after being washed, and made nice and clean, they have others put on to wear all day, but at night they are obliged to have their dirty ones put on again, because their parents are so wicked, that if they went home in good clothes they would take them from them and sell them, and spend the money on something to drink. Then they would send the children out again in miserable and filthy rags, or nearly without clothes at all; so the kind people at the schools take care of the clean clothing for them at night. The children stay at school all day and have food provided for them. Sometimes they have one thing, sometimes another. The day I was at **Dr Guthrie's school**, they had each a basin of nice hot soup and a good-sized piece of bread. What a treat for these poor, neglected, hungry things! Perhaps you, my young friends, never knew what it was to want a morsel of bread. It is a terrible thing to be very hungry and to have nothing to eat; a terrible thing to see the shop windows full of nice bread, and cakes, etc.; to be very, very hungry, and to have no means of obtaining anything but by stealing.

Dr Guthrie's school Thomas Guthrie was the founder of the Ragged Schools

Extract from *Hard Times* by Charles Dickens

In this extract from the novel *Hard Times*, which was first published in 1854, Thomas Gradgrind, the headmaster of a school located in the industrial town of Coketown, tests two of his students.

"Girl number twenty," said Mr. Gradgrind, squarely pointing with his square forefinger, "I don't know that girl. Who is that girl?"

"Sissy Jupe, sir," explained number twenty, blushing, standing up, and curtseying.

"Sissy is not a name," said Mr. Gradgrind. "Don't call yourself Sissy. Call yourself Cecilia."

"It's father as calls me Sissy, sir," returned the young girl in a trembling voice, and with another curtsey.

"Then he has no business to do it," said Mr. Gradgrind. "Tell him he mustn't. Cecilia Jupe. Let me see. What is your father?"

"He belongs to the horse-riding, if you please, sir."

Mr. Gradgrind frowned, and waved off the objectionable calling with his hand.

"We don't want to know anything about that, here.

You mustn't tell us about that, here. Your father breaks horses, don't he?"

"If you please, sir, when they can get any to break, they do break horses in the ring, sir."

"You mustn't tell us about the ring, here. Very well, then. Describe your father as a horsebreaker. He doctors sick horses, I dare say?"

"Oh yes, sir."

"Very well, then. He is a veterinary surgeon, a **farrier**, and horsebreaker. Give me your definition of a horse."

(Sissy Jupe thrown into the greatest alarm by this demand.)

"Girl number twenty unable to define a horse!" said Mr. Gradgrind, for the general behoof of all the little pitchers. "Girl number twenty possessed of no facts, in reference to one of the commonest of animals! Some boy's definition of a horse. Bitzer, yours."

The square finger, moving here and there, lighted suddenly on Bitzer, perhaps because he chanced to sit in the same ray of sunlight which, darting in at one of the bare windows of the intensely white-washed room, **irradiated** Sissy. For, the boys and girls sat on the face of the inclined plane in two compact bodies, divided up the centre by a narrow interval; and Sissy, being at the corner of a row on the sunny side, came in for the beginning of a sunbeam, of which Bitzer, being at the corner of a row on the other side, a few rows in advance, caught the end. But, whereas the girl was so dark-eyed and dark-haired, that she seemed to receive a deeper and more lustrous colour from the sun, when it shone upon her, the boy was so light-eyed and light-haired that the self-same rays appeared to draw out of him what little colour he ever possessed. His cold eyes would hardly have been eyes, but for the short ends of lashes which, by bringing them into immediate contrast with something paler than themselves, expressed their form. His short-cropped hair might have been a mere continuation of the sandy freckles on his forehead and face. His skin was so unwholesomely deficient in the natural tinge, that he looked as though, if he were cut, he would bleed white.

"Bitzer," said Thomas Gradgrind. "Your definition of a horse."

"Quadruped. **Graminivorous**. Forty teeth, namely twenty-four grinders, four eye-teeth, and twelve incisive. Sheds coat in the spring; in marshy countries, sheds hoofs, too. Hoofs hard, but requiring to be shod with iron. Age known by marks in mouth." Thus (and much more) Bitzer.

"Now girl number twenty," said Mr. Gradgrind. "You know what a horse is."

---

farrier a blacksmith who shoes horses
irradiated illuminated
graminivorous an animal that feeds on grain

Extract from a speech by Charles Dickens

Charles Dickens used his fame as a writer to help raise funds to educate poor and less fortunate children. The following extract is taken from the text of a speech that he gave on 5th November 1857, appealing for funds for a school for orphaned children.

Conspicuous on the card of admission to this dinner is the word "Schools." This set me thinking this morning what are the sorts of schools that I don't like. I found them on consideration, to be rather numerous. I don't like to begin with, and to begin as charity does at home – I don't like the sort of school to which I once went myself – the respected **proprietor** of which was by far the most ignorant man I have ever had the pleasure to know; one of the worst-tempered men perhaps that ever lived, whose business it was to make as much out of us and put as little into us as possible, and who sold us at a figure which I remember we used to delight to estimate, as amounting to exactly 2 pounds 4s. 6d. per head.

I don't like that sort of school, because I don't see what business the master had to be at the top of it instead of the bottom. Again, I don't like that sort of school – and I have seen a great many such in these latter times – where the bright childish imagination is utterly discouraged, and where those bright childish faces, which it is so very good for the wisest among us to remember in after life – when the world is too much with us, early and late – are gloomily and grimly scared out of countenance; where I have never seen among the pupils, whether boys or girls, anything but little parrots and small calculating machines. Lastly, I do not like, and I did not like some years ago, cheap distant schools, where neglected children pine from year to year under an amount of neglect, want, and youthful misery far too sad even to be glanced at in this cheerful **assembly**.

And now, ladies and gentlemen, perhaps you will permit me to sketch in a few words the sort of school that I do like. It is a children's school, which is at the same time no less a children's home, a home not to be confided to the care of cold or ignorant strangers, but to be from generation to generation administered by men living in precisely such homes as those poor children have lost; by men always bent upon making that replacement, such a home as their own dear children might find a happy refuge in if they themselves were taken early away. And I fearlessly ask you, is this a design which has any claim to your sympathy? Is this a sort of school which is deserving of your support?

Ladies and gentlemen, this little "labour of love" of mine is now done. I most heartily wish that I could charm you now not to see me, not to think of me, not to hear me – I most heartily wish that I could make you see in my **stead** the multitude of innocent and bereaved children who are looking towards these schools, and **entreating** with uplifted hands to be let in. A very famous **advocate** once said, in speaking of his fears of failure when he had first to speak in court, being very poor, that he felt his little children tugging at his skirts, and that recovered him. Will you think of the number of little children who are tugging at my skirts, when I ask you, in their names, on their behalf, and in their little persons, and in no strength of my own, to encourage and assist this work?

---

conspicuous noticeable
proprietor owner
assembly group of people
stead in place of another person
entreating asking earnestly
advocate lawyer

Extract from *Jane Eyre* by Charlotte Brontë

FICTION

> The following extract from the novel *Jane Eyre*, which was first published in 1847, describes the harsh life at Lowood, a charity school for girls, which Jane has been sent to.

The next day commenced as before, getting up and dressing by **rushlight**; but this morning we were obliged to dispense with the ceremony of washing; the water in the **pitchers** was frozen. A change had taken place in the weather the preceding evening, and a keen north-east wind, whistling through the crevices of our bedroom windows all night long, had made us shiver in our beds, and turned the contents of the **ewers** to ice.

Before the long hour and a half of prayers and Bible-reading was over, I felt ready to perish with cold. Breakfast-time came at last, and this morning the porridge was not burnt; the quality was eatable, the quantity small. How small my portion seemed! I wished it had been doubled.

In the course of the day I was enrolled a member of the fourth class, and regular tasks and occupations were assigned me: **hitherto**, I had only been a spectator of the proceedings at Lowood; I was now to become an actor therein. At first, being little accustomed to learn by heart, the lessons appeared to me both long and difficult; the frequent change from task to task, too, bewildered me; and I was glad when, about three o'clock in the afternoon, Miss Smith put into my hands a border of **muslin** two yards long, together with needle, thimble, etc., and sent me to sit in a quiet corner of the schoolroom, with directions to hem the same. At that hour most of the others were sewing likewise; but one class still stood round Miss Scatcherd's chair reading, and as all was quiet, the subject of their lessons could be heard, together with the manner in which each girl acquitted herself, and the **animadversions** or commendations of Miss Scatcherd on the performance. It was English history: among the readers I observed my acquaintance of the verandah: at the commencement of the lesson, her place had been at the top of the class, but for some error of pronunciation, or some inattention to stops, she was suddenly sent to the very bottom. Even in that obscure position, Miss Scatcherd continued to make her an object of constant notice: she was continually addressing to her such phrases as the following:—

"Burns" (such it seems was her name: the girls here were all called by their surnames, as boys are elsewhere), "Burns, you are standing on the side of your shoe; turn your toes out immediately." "Burns, you poke your chin

11

most unpleasantly; draw it in." "Burns, I insist on your holding your head up; I will not have you before me in that attitude," etc. etc.

A chapter having been read through twice, the books were closed and the girls examined. The lesson had comprised part of the reign of Charles I., and there were sundry questions about tonnage and poundage and ship-money, which most of them appeared unable to answer; still, every little difficulty was solved instantly when it reached Burns: her memory seemed to have retained the substance of the whole lesson, and she was ready with answers on every point. I kept expecting that Miss Scatcherd would praise her attention; but, instead of that, she suddenly cried out—

"You dirty, disagreeable girl! you have never cleaned your nails this morning!"

Burns made no answer: I wondered at her silence. "Why," thought I, "does she not explain that she could neither clean her nails nor wash her face, as the water was frozen?"

My attention was now called off by Miss Smith desiring me to hold a **skein** of thread: while she was winding it, she talked to me from time to time, asking whether I had ever been at school before, whether I could mark, stitch, knit, etc.; till she dismissed me, I could not pursue my observations on Miss Scatcherd's movements. When I returned to my seat, that lady was just delivering an order of which I did not catch the **import**; but Burns immediately left the class, and going into the small inner room where the books were kept, returned in half a minute, carrying in her hand a bundle of twigs tied together at one end. This ominous tool she presented to Miss Scatcherd with a respectful curtesy; then she quietly, and without being told, unloosed her pinafore, and the teacher instantly and sharply inflicted on her neck a dozen strokes with the bunch of twigs. Not a tear rose to Burns' eye; and, while I paused from my sewing, because my fingers quivered at this spectacle with a sentiment of unavailing and impotent anger, not a feature of her pensive face altered its ordinary expression.

"Hardened girl!" exclaimed Miss Scatcherd; "nothing can correct you of your **slatternly** habits: carry the rod away."

Burns obeyed: I looked at her narrowly as she emerged from the book-closet; she was just putting back her handkerchief into her pocket, and the trace of a tear glistened on her thin cheek.

---

rushlight a type of candle
pitchers jugs
hitherto until this time
muslin a type of cotton
animadversions critical remarks
skein a coil of thread
import meaning
slatternly slovenly or untidy

13

Extract from *Walks in and Around London*

This extract is taken from the guidebook *Walks in and Around London*, first published in 1895, and describes a children's playground in the East End of London.

A playground in the east of London, with its throng of children whirling in and out, and jostling one another in their uproarious merriment. It is a scene of constant motion; but with just a little of sadness running through the whole. We seem to look through their merry play and see beyond into the home-life of many of these poor little ones. We, who revel in our cosy nurseries and play-rooms, who tread with slippered feet on soft carpeted floors, who feast our eyes with bright pictures and cheerful books, and who lie snugly tucked in with warm blankets on downy beds, know and feel the full meaning of the word 'Home.' But how different it is with many of these poor little ones of outcast London! To them 'home' is often full of bitterness. Shoeless feet, bare boards, perhaps a few shavings or bits of straw for bed, and rags for coverlets, are their home comforts. They are more used to kicks than kisses, to blows than fond embraces, to angry words and horrible oaths than gentle voices of love and prayer. Money enough is found for the gin and other ruinous drinks, but none for home joys or proper clothing. And the publican thrives, and his children live well and dress in fine clothes with the money that ought to feed and clothe these poor children. And too often, because the children and the drink together cost too much money, and one or other must be given up, the poor children are driven from home. To such this playground is a paradise.

A little while ago this bright spot was a sad, dull and melancholy waste. Maybe it was an old churchyard with every grave filled: its stones, in memory of folks long since forgotten, now crumbling with age; and railed in all round to keep out children, large and small. But wise and kind-hearted people have levelled and laid it out as a garden and playground for the little ones. Here, strolling along its sanded walks, which go winding a round beds of bright-looking and sweet-smelling flowers; or stopping to watch the jet of water flung into the air from the fountain and dropping back into the basin where the gold and silver fish dart to and fro; or leaning back in the comfortable seats like real ladies and gentlemen, the myriads of children from the courts and alleys around, as well as those just let out from school, come to forget the hardness of their life in the beauty and merriment of the playground.

Some of you whose friends bring you so many grand toys, would not look at the things that bring these poor children such enjoyment. An old shuttlecock with one solitary feather in it, picked up from some dust-heap, is batted into the air with a piece of cardboard. A paper Windmill bought for a farthing, which mother has squeezed out of her hard earnings, delights that little three-year-old boy as he holds it tightly in his chubby fist. His clothes are ragged and torn, yet I'm sure his mother is kind to him. He has found out that by holding the mill straight in front of him, the wind catches the bright-coloured sails and spins them round till the colours run one into the other and he sees only a rainbow-coloured ring in front of him. So, forgetting the big boots shaking about on his feet, he trots up and down, laughing so merrily.

How admiringly one ragged little fellow looks on at the toy! He, poor boy, never had such a toy to make him happy. He likes to see the whizzing wheel; but rougher games amongst the courts and alleys suit him best. He is one of those little urchins who in the dark days of winter startle us so with their shrill calls, or who so suddenly appear at our sides begging a '**copper**.' If we speak to him, he will call us 'general' or 'captain,' at the same time saluting us while his eyes twinkle roguishly. Poor little chap! Of course he gets his copper; for his life is a hard one. He dares not creep in to rest at night until the gin palaces are shut, and he knows his parents are sleeping their drunken sleep. Still he looks for a bit of play in this playground. Bits of string picked from the shop sweepings and tied together, serve to start him: and in a twinkling he is the happy driver of a couple of boys who prance about as only carriage horses can; or the furious driver of a fire-engine; or managing the swift steeds in a race, just as fancy suits him.

Here, with pale faces and wasted limbs, are the cripples, limping painfully along on crutches, admiring the lovely flowers; or seated to watch the joyous games of their companions. Breathing the air made sweet by the flowers, and drinking in the enjoyment of the others, their cheeks lose their paleness, their eyes their heaviness, and the sadness of their sufferings is forgotten in the gladness of the hour spent in the playground.

Here, too, come the little mothers carrying babies, and looking after brothers and sisters with as much care and anxiety as though they were real mothers. And the little workers with busy fingers stitch and knit and crochet the articles which mother gets from the warehouse, and which must be worked at early and late to earn money enough to live.

And so we leave this happy scene, glad that the poor children have this fine place of enjoyment. And when we romp about in our comfortable homes and play with our toys, we will think kindly of these poor little ones, and, when opportunity comes, will help them as best we can.

---

copper a small coin

Letter to *The Times* newspaper

In the 19th century one popular children's game was to roll a hoop with a stick. However this game wasn't without dangers as this letter published in *The Times* newspaper on 1st October 1842 illustrates.

THE HOOP NUISANCE

Sir, I have not for many years read a paragraph in *The Times* which has afforded me greater pleasure than that which heads your "Police" report of this day, conveying Mr. Hardwick's just complaint of, and directions to Inspector Baker, on the hoop nuisance. As a daily passenger along the crowded thoroughfares of London-bridge and Thames-street, where boys and even girls, drive their hoops as deliberately as if upon a clear and open common, I can bear witness to its danger and inconvenience. I have at this moment a large scar on one of my shins, the legacy of a severe wound, which festered, and was very painful for an entire month, inflicted a year ago by the iron hoop of a **whey-faced, cadaverous charity-boy** from Tower-hill, who on my remonstrating with him on his carelessness, added impudence to the injury, by significantly advancing his extended fingers and thumb to his nose and scampering off. Aware that I had no redress, that the police would not interfere, I was compelled to grin and bear it while I hobbled away. The nuisance calls loudly for the interference of the Police Commissioners.

Your daily reader,
A PEDESTRIAN.

whey-faced pale
cadaverous corpselike
charity-boy a boy who attends a charity school for the very poor

Extract from *The Mill on the Floss* by George Eliot

> The following extract is taken from the novel *The Mill on the Floss*, which was first published in 1860. Here, a boy called Tom falls into an argument with his friend Bob, who comes from a poorer family.

"Ah, and I should have halfpence, and we'd play at heads-and-tails," said Tom, not contemplating the possibility that this recreation might have fewer charms for his mature age. "I'd divide fair to begin with, and then we'd see who'd win."

"I've got a halfpenny o' my own," said Bob, proudly, coming out of the water and tossing his halfpenny in the air. "Yeads or tails?"

"Tails," said Tom, instantly fired with the desire to win.

"It's yeads," said Bob, hastily, snatching up the halfpenny as it fell.

"It wasn't," said Tom, loudly and **peremptorily**. "You give me the halfpenny; I've won it fair."

"I sha'n't," said Bob, holding it tight in his pocket.

"Then I'll make you; see if I don't," said Tom.

"Yes, I can."

"You can't make me do nothing, you can't," said Bob.

"No, you can't."

"I'm master."

"I don't care for you."

"But I'll make you care, you cheat," said Tom, collaring Bob and shaking him.

"You get out wi' you," said Bob, giving Tom a kick.

Tom's blood was thoroughly up: he went at Bob with a lunge and threw him down, but Bob seized hold and kept it like a cat, and pulled Tom down after him. They struggled fiercely on the ground for a moment or two, till Tom, pinning Bob down by the shoulders, thought he had the mastery.

"*You*, say you'll give me the halfpenny now," he said, with difficulty, while he exerted himself to keep the command of Bob's arms.

But at this moment Yap, who had been running on before, returned barking to the scene of action, and saw a favourable opportunity for biting Bob's bare leg not only with impunity but with honour. The pain from Yap's teeth, instead of surprising Bob into a relaxation of his hold, gave it a fiercer tenacity, and with a new exertion of his force he pushed Tom backward and got uppermost. But now Yap, who could get no sufficient purchase before, set his teeth in a new place, so that Bob, harassed in this way, let go his hold of Tom, and, almost throttling

Yap, flung him into the river. By this time Tom was up again, and before Bob had quite recovered his balance after the act of swinging Yap, Tom fell upon him, threw him down, and got his knees firmly on Bob's chest.

"You give me the halfpenny now," said Tom.

"Take it," said Bob, sulkily.

"No, I sha'n't take it; you give it me."

Bob took the halfpenny out of his pocket, and threw it away from him on the ground.

Tom loosed his hold, and left Bob to rise.

"There the halfpenny lies," he said. "I don't want your halfpenny; I wouldn't have kept it. But you wanted to cheat; I hate a cheat. I sha'n't go along with you any more," he added, turning round homeward, not without casting a regret toward the rat-catching and other pleasures which he must **relinquish** along with Bob's society.

"You may let it alone, then," Bob called out after him. "I shall cheat if I like; there's no fun i' playing else; and I know where there's a goldfinch's nest, but I'll take care *you* don't. An' you're a nasty fightin' turkey-cock, you are—"

Tom walked on without looking around, and Yap followed his example, the cold bath having moderated his passions.

"Go along wi' you, then, wi' your drowned dog; I wouldn't own such a dog – *I* wouldn't," said Bob, getting louder, in a last effort to sustain his defiance. But Tom was not to be provoked into turning round, and Bob's voice began to falter a little as he said,–

"An' I'n gi'en you everything, an' showed you everything, an' niver wanted nothin' from you. An' there's your horn-handed knife, then as you gi'en me." Here Bob flung the knife as far as he could after Tom's retreating footsteps. But it produced no effect, except the sense in Bob's mind that there was a terrible void in his lot, now that knife was gone.

peremptorily not allowing a refusal
relinquish to give something up

Extract from *Tom Brown's Schooldays* by Thomas Hughes

The following extract is taken from the novel *Tom Brown's Schooldays*, which was first published in 1860. This novel is set at Rugby School, an independent school for boys, and the events described take place in the 1830s. Here, Tom defends his friend Arthur from a bully named Slogger Williams.

Tom was detained in school a few minutes after the rest, and on coming out into the quadrangle, the first thing he saw was a small ring of boys, applauding Williams, who was holding Arthur by the collar.

"There, you young sneak," said he, giving Arthur a cuff on the head with his other hand; "what made you say that—"

"Hullo!" said Tom, shouldering into the crowd; "you drop that, Williams; you shan't touch him."

"Who'll stop me?" said the Slogger, raising his hand again.

"I," said Tom; and suiting the action to the word he struck the arm which held Arthur's arm so sharply that the Slogger dropped it with a start, and turned the full current of his wrath on Tom.

"Will you fight?"

"Yes, of course."

"Huzza! There's going to be a fight between Slogger Williams and Tom Brown!"

The news ran like wildfire about, and many boys who were on their way to tea at their several houses turned back, and sought the back of the chapel, where the fights come off.

"Just run and tell East to come and back me," said Tom to a small School-house boy, who was off like a rocket to Harrowell's, just stopping for a moment to poke his head into the School-house hall, where the lower boys were already at tea, and sing out, "Fight! Tom Brown and Slogger Williams."

Up start half the boys at once, leaving bread, eggs, butter, sprats, and all the rest to take care of themselves. The greater part of the remainder follow in a minute, after swallowing their tea, carrying their food in their hands to consume as they go. Three or four only remain, who steal the butter of the more impetuous, and make to themselves an unctuous feast.

In another minute East and Martin tear through the quadrangle, carrying a sponge, and arrive at the scene of action just as the combatants are beginning to strip.

Tom felt he had got his work cut out for him, as he stripped off his jacket, waistcoat, and braces. East tied his handkerchief round his waist, and rolled up his shirtsleeves for him. "Now, old boy, don't you open your mouth to say a word, or try to help yourself a bit—we'll do all that; you keep all your breath and strength for the Slogger." Martin meanwhile folded the clothes, and put them under the chapel rails; and now Tom, with East to handle him, and Martin to give him a knee, steps out on the turf, and is ready for all that may come; and here is the Slogger too, all stripped, and thirsting for the fray.

It doesn't look a fair match at first glance: Williams is nearly two inches taller, and probably a long year older than his opponent, and he is very strongly made about the arms and shoulders—"peels well," as the little knot of big fifth-form boys, the amateurs, say, who stand outside the ring of little boys, looking complacently on, but taking no active part in the proceedings. But down below he is not so good by any means—no spring from the loins, and feeblish, not to say shipwrecky, about the knees. Tom, on the contrary, though not half so strong in the arms, is good all over, straight, hard, and springy, from neck to ankle, better perhaps in his legs than anywhere. Besides, you can see by the clear white of his eye, and fresh, bright look of his skin, that he is in tip-top training, able to do all he knows; while the Slogger looks rather sodden, as if he didn't take much exercise and ate too much tuck. The time-keeper is chosen, a large ring made, and the two stand up opposite one another for a moment, giving us time just to make our little observations.

"If Tom'll only condescend to fight with his head and heels," as East mutters to Martin, "we shall do."

But seemingly he won't, for there he goes in, making play with both hands. Hard all is the word; the two stand to one another like men; rally follows rally in quick succession, each fighting as if he thought to finish the whole thing out of hand. "Can't last at this rate," say the knowing ones, while the partisans of each make the air ring with their shouts and counter-shouts of encouragement, approval, and defiance.

"Take it easy, take it easy; keep away; let him come after you," implores East, as he wipes Tom's face after the first round with a wet sponge, while he sits back on Martin's knee, supported by the Madman's long arms which tremble a little from excitement.

"Time's up," calls the time-keeper.

"There he goes again, hang it all!" growls East, as his man is at it again, as hard as ever. A very severe round follows, in which Tom gets out and out the worst of it, and is at last hit clean off his legs, and deposited on the grass by a right-hander from the Slogger.

Loud shouts rise from the boys of Slogger's house, and the School-house are silent and vicious, ready to pick quarrels anywhere.

Men and women

Men and women were not treated equally in the 19th century. Although a woman, Queen Victoria, sat on the British throne for most of the century, it was men who held the power in almost all areas of society. Women weren't allowed to vote and, until 1882, married women weren't even allowed to own their own property, with all of a woman's possessions becoming her husband's legal property from the moment they married. Getting divorced was an expensive process and one that could only be afforded by the wealthiest of men.

Victorian society was obsessed with status and one of the few ways for a woman to improve her position in society was by marrying a wealthy husband. Etiquette guides presented aspiring social climbers with advice on the expected rules of behaviour in upper-class circles, detailing what to wear, how to speak and even when to kiss. Anyone who didn't measure up to these rules could find themselves looked down upon or even treated harshly by those of a higher social status.

Extract from *Pride and Prejudice* by Jane Austen

In Victorian society one of the only ways a young woman could improve her fortunes was by marrying a wealthy husband. The following extract is taken from the opening to the novel *Pride and Prejudice*, which was first published in 1813. Here, Mrs Bennet informs Mr Bennet that the neighbouring manor of Netherfield Park has been rented by a young gentleman who Mrs Bennet hopes might be interested in marrying one of her five daughters.

It is a truth universally acknowledged, that a single man in possession of a good fortune, must be in want of a wife.

However little known the feelings or views of such a man may be on his first entering a neighbourhood, this truth is so well fixed in the minds of the surrounding families, that he is considered the rightful property of some one or other of their daughters.

"My dear Mr. Bennet," said his lady to him one day, "have you heard that Netherfield Park is let at last?"

Mr. Bennet replied that he had not.

"But it is," returned she; "for Mrs. Long has just been here, and she told me all about it."

Mr. Bennet made no answer.

"Do you not want to know who has taken it?" cried his wife impatiently.

"*You* want to tell me, and I have no objection to hearing it."

This was invitation enough.

"Why, my dear, you must know, Mrs. Long says that Netherfield is taken by a young man of large fortune from the north of England; that he came down on Monday in a chaise and four to see the place, and was so much delighted with it, that he agreed with Mr. Morris immediately; that he is to take possession before Michaelmas, and some of his servants are to be in the house by the end of next week."

"What is his name?"

"Bingley."

"Is he married or single?"

"Oh! Single, my dear, to be sure! A single man of large fortune; four or five thousand a year. What a fine thing for our girls!"

"How so? How can it affect them?"

"My dear Mr. Bennet," replied his wife, "how can you be so tiresome! You must know that I am thinking of his marrying one of them."

"Is that his **design** in settling here?"

"Design! Nonsense, how can you talk so! But it is very likely that he *may* fall in love with one of them, and therefore you must visit him as soon as he comes."

"I see no occasion for that. You and the girls may go, or you may send them by themselves, which perhaps will be still better, for as you are as handsome as any of them, Mr. Bingley may like you the best of the party."

"My dear, you flatter me. I certainly *have* had my share of beauty, but I do not pretend to be anything extraordinary now. When a woman has five grown-up daughters, she ought to give over thinking of her own beauty."

"In such cases, a woman has not often much beauty to think of."

"But, my dear, you must indeed go and see Mr. Bingley when he comes into the neighbourhood."

"It is more than I engage for, I assure you."

"But consider your daughters. Only think what an establishment it would be for one of them. Sir William and Lady Lucas are determined to go, merely on that account, for in general, you know, they visit no newcomers. Indeed you must go, for it will be impossible for *us* to visit him if you do not."

"You are over-scrupulous, surely. I dare say Mr. Bingley will be very glad to see you; and I will send a few lines by you to assure him of my hearty consent to his marrying whichever he chooses of the girls; though I must throw in a good word for my little Lizzy."

"I desire you will do no such thing. Lizzy is not a bit better than the others; and I am sure she is not half so handsome as Jane, nor half so good-humoured as Lydia. But you are always giving *her* the preference."

"They have none of them much to recommend them," replied he; "they are all silly and ignorant like other girls; but Lizzy has something more of quickness than her sisters."

"Mr. Bennet, how *can* you abuse your own children in such a way? You take delight in vexing me. You have no compassion for my poor nerves."

"You mistake me, my dear. I have a high respect for your nerves. They are my old friends. I have heard you mention them with consideration these last twenty years at least."

"Ah, you do not know what I suffer."

"But I hope you will get over it, and live to see many young men of four thousand a year come into the neighbourhood."

"It will be no use to us, if twenty such should come, since you will not visit them."

"Depend upon it, my dear, that when there are twenty, I will visit them all."

design plan

Extract from *Our Deportment* by John H. Young

> In Victorian society, men and women were expected to act in certain ways. The following extract describes how men and women should greet each other and is taken from *Our Deportment*, an etiquette guide published in 1881.

WORDS OF SALUTATION.

The words commonly used in **saluting** a person are "Good Morning," "Good Afternoon," "Good Evening," "How do you do" and "How are you." The three former are most appropriate, as it seems somewhat absurd to ask after a person's health, unless you stop to receive an answer. A respectful bow should accompany the words.

SHAKING HANDS.

Among friends the shaking of the hand is the most genuine and cordial expression of good-will. It is not necessary, though in certain cases it is not forbidden, upon introduction; but when acquaintanceship has reached any degree of intimacy, it is perfectly proper.

ETIQUETTE OF HANDSHAKING.

An authority upon this subject says: "The etiquette of handshaking is simple. A man has no right to take a lady's hand until it is offered. He has even less right to pinch or retain it. Two young ladies shake hands gently and softly. A young lady gives her hand, but does not shake a gentleman's unless she is his friend. A lady should always rise to give her hand; a gentleman, of course, never dares to do so seated."

In shaking hands, the right hand should always be offered, unless it be so engaged as to make it impossible, and then an excuse should be offered. The French give the left hand, as nearest the heart.

The mistress of a household should offer her hand to every guest invited to her house.

A gentleman must not shake hands with a lady until she has made the first move in that direction. It is a mark of rudeness not to give his hand instantly, should she extend her own. A married lady should always extend her hand to a stranger brought to her house by a common friend, as an evidence of her cordial welcome. Where an introduction is for dancing there is no shaking of hands.

THE KISS.

This is the most affectionate form of **salutation**, and is only proper among near relations and dear friends.

THE KISS OF FRIENDSHIP.

The kiss of friendship and relationship is on the cheeks and forehead. In this country this act of affection is generally excluded from public eyes, and in the case of parents and children and near relations, it is perhaps unnecessarily so.

KISSING IN PUBLIC.

The custom which has become quite prevalent of women kissing each other whenever they meet in public, is regarded as vulgar, and by ladies of delicacy and refinement is entirely avoided.

saluting, salutation greeting

Extract from *Daisy Miller* by Henry James

> The following extract is taken from the novel *Daisy Miller*, which was first published in 1878. Here, a young man named Frederick Winterbourne is telling his aunt about Daisy Miller, a young American girl he has just met. However, Frederick discovers that his aunt disapproves of Daisy.

"They are very common," Mrs. Costello declared. "They are the sort of Americans that one does one's duty by not—not accepting."

"Ah, you don't accept them?" said the young man.

"I can't, my dear Frederick. I would if I could, but I can't."

"The young girl is very pretty," said Winterbourne in a moment.

"Of course she's pretty. But she is very common."

"I see what you mean, of course," said Winterbourne after another pause.

"She has that charming look that they all have," his aunt resumed. "I can't think where they pick it up; and she dresses in perfection—no, you don't know how well she dresses. I can't think where they get their taste."

"But, my dear aunt, she is not, after all, a **Comanche savage**."

"She is a young lady," said Mrs. Costello, "who has an intimacy with her mamma's **courier**."

"An intimacy with the courier?" the young man demanded.

"Oh, the mother is just as bad! They treat the courier like a familiar friend—like a gentleman. I shouldn't wonder if he dines with them. Very likely they have never seen a man with such good manners, such fine clothes, so like a gentleman. He probably corresponds to the young lady's idea of a count. He sits with them in the garden in the evening. I think he smokes."

Winterbourne listened with interest to these disclosures; they helped him to make up his mind about Miss Daisy. Evidently she was rather wild. "Well," he said, "I am not a courier, and yet she was very charming to me."

"You had better have said at first," said Mrs. Costello with dignity, "that you had made her acquaintance."

"We simply met in the garden, and we talked a bit."

"**Tout bonnement**! And pray what did you say?"

"I said I should take the liberty of introducing her to my admirable aunt."

"I am much obliged to you."

"It was to guarantee my respectability," said Winterbourne.

"And pray who is to guarantee hers?"

"Ah, you are cruel!" said the young man. "She's a very nice young girl."

"You don't say that as if you believed it," Mrs. Costello observed.

"She is completely uncultivated," Winterbourne went on. "But she is wonderfully pretty, and, in short, she is very nice. To prove that I believe it, I am going to take her to the Chateau de Chillon."

"You two are going off there together? I should say it proved just the contrary. How long had you known her, may I ask, when this interesting project was formed? You haven't been twenty-four hours in the house."

"I have known her half an hour!" said Winterbourne, smiling.

"Dear me!" cried Mrs. Costello. "What a dreadful girl!"

Comanche savage Native American
courier personal attendant hired to make travel arrangements
tout bonnement a French expression meaning 'simply'

Article from *Punch* magazine

> The following article was published in *Punch* magazine in 1844 and provides some humorous advice for husbands on how to behave in the home.

HINTS TO MAKE HOME HAPPY – TO HUSBANDS

KEEP up the practice of reading the paper during the whole of breakfast time; of allowing yourself to be spoken to half-a-dozen times before you answer, and then of asking your wife what it was that she said. Upon her telling you, make some reply which is nothing to the purpose, as if you were thinking of something else.

Having been out over night at an evening party, which your wife was prevented from going to by indisposition, entertain her the next morning by a minute description of the young lady you danced with, **descanting** on every point as enthusiastically as possible.

Take frequent opportunities of praising features and personal peculiarities which are as different as possible from your wife's. For instance, if she has blue eyes, say how you like black; if dark hair, how much you admire light; if she is tall, remark that you prefer a moderate height; and if short, be constantly quoting Byron, to the effect that you "hate a dumpy woman".

Some wives are very particular about their **fenders**. Should this be the case with yours, always use it for your footstool. When fresh **drugget** has been laid down on the stairs, particularly if it is a rainy day, invariably forget to scrape your shoes.

Discover, frequently, on a cold raw morning, that the room is close, and insist on having the windows open. On the other hand, be as often, during the height of the dog-days, affected with a chilliness, which shall oblige you to keep them shut.

Very often order dinner punctually at five, and very seldom come home till a quarter to six. Occasionally, however, return at the appointed hour, and, not finding things ready, complain that you are never attended to.

If your fish, your joint, or your vegetables, should happen accidentally to be a little under or over done, never smother your disappointment like some people, but express it as markedly as you can, and remain in an ill humour for the rest of the evening. Be never quite satisfied with what is set before you; but, if possible, find some fault with every dish; or, if not, quarrel with the arrangements of the table. If you can find nothing else to grumble at, think of something that you would have liked better than what has been got for you, and say so.

Wives occasionally make pies and puddings, with a view to a little **approbation**. Never bestow this, on any account; but always say you wished these things were left to the cook.

Knowing that there is nothing but cold meat in the house, bring home, every now and then, half-a-dozen men, unexpectedly, to take **pot-luck** with you. Your wife will probably sit at table flurried and uncomfortable; in which case, amuse them by joking at her expense.

Should you chance, after dinner, to be affected by a slight drowsiness, never resist it because your wife wishes to chat with you; do not mind her, but go quietly to sleep.

When you have an evening party at your house, come home to dress just as the company is beginning to arrive.

Should you find yourself at eleven o'clock at night among a set of bachelor friends, and be offered a cigar, always stay and smoke it, and another after it if you like, and, if you please, another after that; in fact, as many as you find agreeable; never troubling yourself for an instant about keeping your wife and the servants up.

In short, on all occasions, consult studiously your own inclinations, and indulge, without the least restriction, your every whim and **caprice**; but never regard your wife's feelings at all; still less make the slightest allowance for any weakness or peculiarity of her character; and your home will assuredly be as happy as you deserve that it should be.

---

descanting discussing at length
fenders a type of cushion
drugget a type of rug
approbation praise
pot-luck a meal prepared from whatever food is available
caprice an impulsive change of mind

Extract from *In the Year of the Jubilee* by George Gissing

The idea of marrying someone from a poorer background or lower social class was frowned upon in Victorian society. In this extract from the novel *In the Year of the Jubilee*, first published in 1894, a young man called Horace Lord has just informed his father that he plans to marry Miss French, a young woman from a lower social class.

"You really imagine," said his father, "that I should give you money to enable you to marry that idiot?"

Evidently he put a severe restraint upon himself. The veins of his temples were congested; his nostrils grew wide; and he spoke rather hoarsely. Horace straightened his back, and, though in great fear, strung himself for conflict.

"I don't see—what right—to insult the young lady."

His father took him up sternly.

"Young lady? What do you mean by 'young lady'? After all your education, haven't you learnt to distinguish a lady from a dressed-up kitchen wench? *I* had none of your advantages. There was—there would have been some excuse for *me*, if I had made such a fool of myself.

What were you doing all those years at school, if it wasn't learning the difference between real and sham, getting to understand things better than poor folks' children? You disappointed me, and a good deal more than I ever told you. I had hoped you would come from school better able to make a place in the world than your father was. I made up my mind long ago that you should never go into my business; you were to be something a good deal better. But after all you couldn't, or wouldn't, do what I wanted. Never mind—I said to myself—never mind; at all events, he has learnt to *think* in a better way than if I had sent him to common schools, and after all that's the main thing. But here you come to me and talk of marrying a low-bred, low-minded creature, who wouldn't be good enough for the meanest clerk!"

"How do you know that, father? What—what right have you to say such things, without knowing more of her than you do?"

There was a brief silence before Mr. Lord spoke again.

"You are very young," he said, with less vehement contempt. "I must remember that. At your age, a lad has a sort of devil in him, that's always driving him out of the path of common sense, whether he will or no. I'll try my best to talk quietly with you. Does your sister know what has been going on?"

"I daresay she does. I haven't told her in so many words."

"I never thought of it," pursued Mr. Lord gloomily. "I took it for granted that everybody must see those people as I myself did. I have wondered now and then why Nancy kept up any kind of acquaintance with them, but she spoke of them in the rational way, and that seemed enough. I may have thought that they might get some sort of good out of *her*, and I felt sure she had too much sense to get harm from *them*. If it hadn't been so, I should have forbidden her to know them at all. What have you to say for yourself? I don't want to think worse of you than I need. I can make allowance for your age, as I said. What do you see in that girl? Just talk to me freely and plainly."

"After all you have said," replied Horace, his voice still shaky, "what's the use? You seem to be convinced that there isn't a single good quality in her."

"So I am. What I want to know is, what good *you* have found."

"A great deal, else I shouldn't have asked her to marry me."

A vein of stubbornness, unmistakable inheritance from Stephen Lord, had begun to appear in the youth's speech and bearing. He kept his head bent, and moved it a little from side to side.

"Do you think her an exception in the family, then?"

"She's a great deal better in every way than her sisters. But I don't think as badly of them as you do."

Mr. Lord stepped to the door, and out into the passage, where he shouted in his deep voice "Nancy!" The girl quickly appeared.

"Shut the door, please," said her father. All three were now standing about the room.

"Your brother has brought me a piece of news. It ought to interest you, I should think. He wants to marry, and out of all the world, he has chosen Miss. French—the youngest." Horace's position was trying. He did not know what to do with his hands, and he kept balancing now on one foot, now on the other. Nancy had her eyes averted from him, but she met her father's look gravely.

"Now, I want to ask you," Mr. Lord proceeded, "whether you consider Miss. French a suitable wife for your brother? Just give me a plain yes or no."

"I certainly don't," replied the girl, barely subduing the tremor of her voice.

"Both my children are not fools, thank Heaven! Now tell me, if you can, what fault you have to find with the 'young lady,' as your brother calls her?"

"For one thing, I don't think her Horace's equal. She can't really be called a lady."

"You are listening?"

Horace bit his lip in **mortification**, and again his head swung doggedly from side to side.

"We might pass over that," added Mr. Lord. "What about her character? Is there any good point in her?"

"I don't think she means any harm. But she's silly, and I've often thought her selfish."

"You are listening?"

Horace lost patience.

"Then why do you pretend to be friends with her?" he demanded almost fiercely.

"I don't," replied his sister, with a note of disdain. "We knew each other at school, and we haven't altogether broken off, that's all."

"It isn't all!" shouted the young man on a high key. "If you're not friendly with her and her sisters, you've been a great hypocrite. It's only just lately you have begun to think yourself too good for them. They used to come here, and you went to them; and you talked just like friends would do. It's abominable to turn round like this, for the sake of taking father's side against me!"

Mr. Lord regarded his son contemptuously. There was a rather long silence; he spoke at length with severe deliberation.

"When you are ten years older, you'll know a good deal more about young women as they're turned out in these times. You'll have heard the talk of men who have been fools enough to marry choice specimens. When common sense has a chance of getting in a word with you, you'll understand what I now tell you. Wherever you look now-a-days there's sham and rottenness; but the most worthless creature living is one of these trashy, flashy girls,—the kind of girl you see everywhere, high and low,—calling themselves 'ladies,'—thinking themselves too good for any honest, womanly work. Town and country, it's all the same. They're educated; oh yes, they're educated! What sort of wives do they make, with their education? What sort of mothers are they? Before long, there'll be no such thing as a home. They don't know what the word means."

mortification shame

Article from *The Sheffield and Rotherham Independent* newspaper

NON-FICTION

In Victorian times, divorce was an option only open to wealthy married men, with married women treated as second-class citizens. The following newspaper article from *The Sheffield and Rotherham Independent*, published on 29th July 1879, reports on a man who decided to sell his wife instead.

Selling a Wife by Auction

It is only a few months since that a paragraph went the round of the papers relating how a certain stonemason at Rawtenstall, in Rossendale, sold his wife to another man for the sum of £10; but it would seem from certain proceedings which took place last week at Stacksteads, a Rossendale village, that the money value of wives has sadly declined since that event.

A navvy, living at Tunstead Mill, Stacksteads, determined to get rid of the 'partner of his joys and sorrows' by offering her for sale by auction, the highest bidder as usual to take 'the lot.'

On Tuesday last the sale took place at the husband's house, but, despite **Solomon**'s testimony as to a woman being more precious than rubies, and notwithstanding that the spectators were numerous, the highest offer was only 4d, at which low figure the wife was eventually 'knocked down' to another navvy, who, by-the-by, lived next door.

The seller wanted to 'throw in' three children, but the buyer objected, and the bairns were left on hand. The wife, however, went joyfully to the home of her new owner, and seemed to be quite as glad to get away from her late liege lord as he was to part with her.

The occurrence has caused quite a stir in the locality, and has been commented upon by the local press.

Solomon a Biblical figure

Extract from *The Mayor of Casterbridge* by Thomas Hardy

In the following extract from the opening chapter of the novel *The Mayor of Casterbridge*, first published in 1886, a drunken man called Michael Henchard decides to sell his wife, Susan.

"Will anybody buy her?" said the man.

"I wish somebody would," said she firmly. "Her present owner is not at all to her liking!"

"Nor you to mine," said he. "So we are agreed about that. Gentlemen, you hear? It's an agreement to part. She shall take the girl if she wants to, and go her ways. I'll take my tools, and go my ways. 'Tis simple as Scripture history. Now then, stand up, Susan, and show yourself."

"Don't, my **chiel**," whispered a buxom **staylace** dealer in voluminous petticoats, who sat near the woman; "yer good man don't know what he's saying."

The woman, however, did stand up. "Now, who's auctioneer?" cried the hay-trusser.

"I be," promptly answered a short man, with a nose resembling a copper knob, a damp voice, and eyes like button-holes. "Who'll make an offer for this lady?"

The woman looked on the ground, as if she maintained her position by a supreme effort of will.

"Five shillings," said someone, at which there was a laugh.

"No insults," said the husband. "Who'll say a **guinea**?"

Nobody answered; and the female dealer in staylaces interposed.

"Behave yerself moral, good man, for Heaven's love! Ah, what a cruelty is the poor soul married to! Bed and board is dear at some figures 'pon my 'vation 'tis!"

"Set it higher, auctioneer," said the trusser.

"Two guineas!" said the auctioneer; and no one replied.

"If they don't take her for that, in ten seconds they'll have to give more," said the husband. "Very well. Now auctioneer, add another."

"Three guineas—going for three guineas!" said the rheumy man.

"No bid?" said the husband. "Good Lord, why she's cost me fifty times the money, if a penny. Go on."

"Four guineas!" cried the auctioneer.

"I'll tell ye what—I won't sell her for less than five," said the husband, bringing down his fist so that the basins danced. "I'll sell her for five guineas to any man that will pay me the money, and treat her well; and he shall have her for ever, and never hear aught o' me. But she shan't go for less. Now then—five guineas—and she's yours. Susan, you agree?"

She bowed her head with absolute indifference.

"Five guineas," said the auctioneer, "or she'll be withdrawn. Do anybody give it? The last time. Yes or no?"

"Yes," said a loud voice from the doorway.

All eyes were turned. Standing in the triangular opening which formed the door of the tent was a sailor, who, unobserved by the rest, had arrived there within the last two or three minutes. A dead silence followed his affirmation.

"You say you do?" asked the husband, staring at him.

"I say so," replied the sailor.

"Saying is one thing, and paying is another. Where's the money?"

The sailor hesitated a moment, looked anew at the woman, came in, unfolded five crisp pieces of paper, and threw them down upon the tablecloth. They were Bank-of-England notes for five pounds. Upon the face of this he clinked down the shillings severally—one, two, three, four, five.

---

chiel a dialect word for child
staylace a type of lace
guinea a gold coin worth one pound and one shilling

The world of work

As the Industrial Revolution gathered pace in the 19th century new jobs were created in factories, mines and mills. Many of these jobs were carried out by children – sometimes as young as five – who worked in horrendous conditions for extremely low pay. These dangerous jobs led to many deaths and it was only in the mid-19th century that the government passed a law forbidding children beneath the age of ten from working down a mine, but child labour continued in other forms up to the dawn of the 20th century.

For educated women employment opportunities were limited. In contrast to the careers that men could choose, only certain jobs were viewed as being suitable for young educated women and many found employment as governesses, teaching children from wealthy families. In polite society, a woman's place was seen as being in the home, but by the century's end many young women were asserting their right to pursue careers in fields such as science, law and medicine.

Extract from a letter by Thomas Carlyle

> The following extract is taken from a letter written on 11th August 1824. Here, the author describes to his brother, Alexander, a visit he made to the Black Country, a heavily industrialised area to the north and west of Birmingham, where the large number of factories, mills and mines caused a high level of air pollution.

I was one day through the iron and coal works of this neighbourhood, – a half-frightful scene! A space perhaps of 30 square miles, to the north of us, covered over with furnaces, rolling-mills, steam-engines and sooty men. A dense cloud of **pestilential** smoke hangs over it forever, blackening even the grain that grows upon it; and at night the whole region burns like a volcano spitting fire from a thousand tubes of brick. But oh the wretched hundred and fifty thousand mortals that grind out their destiny there! In the coal-mines they were literally naked, many of them, all but trousers; black as ravens; plashing about among dripping caverns, or scrambling amid heaps of broken mineral; and thirsting unquenchably for beer.

In the iron-mills it was little better: blast-furnaces were roaring like the voice of many whirlwinds all around; the fiery metal was hissing thro' its moulds, or sparkling and spitting under hammers of a monstrous size, which fell like so many little earthquakes. Here they were wheeling charred coals, breaking their ironstone, and tumbling all into their fiery pit; there they were turning and boring cannon with a hideous shrieking noise such as the earth could hardly parallel; and through the whole, half-naked demons pouring with sweat and besmeared with soot were hurrying to and fro in their red nightcaps and sheet-iron breeches rolling or hammering or squeezing their glowing metal as if it had been wax or dough. They also had a thirst for ale. Yet on the whole I am told they are very happy: they make forty shillings or more per week, and few of them will work on Mondays. It is in a spot like this that one sees the sources of British power.

---

pestilential poisonous

Extract from workers' testimonies

In the first half of the 19th century, children could be found working in factories, mills and mines. The following extract is taken from the evidence given by young workers to Parliamentary enquiries into the conditions they worked under.

Mary Barrett, 14 years old:

'I have worked down in pit five years; father is working in next pit; I have 12 brothers and sisters – all of them but one live at home; they weave, and wind, and hurry, and one is a counter, one of them can read, none of the rest can, or write; they never went to day-school, but three of them go to Sunday-school; I hurry for my brother John, and come down at seven o'clock about; I go up at six, sometimes seven; I do not like working in pit, but I am obliged to get a living; I work always without stockings, or shoes, or trousers; I wear nothing but my chemise; I have to go up to the headings with the men; they are all naked there; I am got well used to that, and don't care now much about it; I was afraid at first, and did not like it; they never behave rudely to me; I cannot read or write.'

Testimony gathered by Ashley's Mines Commission, 1842

Hannah Goode:

'I work at Mr. Wilson's mill. I think the youngest child is about 7. I daresay there are 20 under 9 years. It is about half past five by our clock at home when we go in… We come out at seven by the mill. We never stop to take our meals, except at dinner. William Crookes is **overlooker** in our room. He is cross-tempered sometimes. He does not beat me; he beats the little children if they do not do their work right. I have sometimes seen the little children drop asleep or so, but not lately. If they are catched asleep they get the strap. They are always very tired at night. I can read a little; I can't write. I used to go to school before I went to the mill; I have since I am sixteen.'

Testimony gathered by Factory Inquiry Commission, 1833

---

overlooker superintendent
pawn pawn shop

Extract from a guidebook to London

This extract from an 1895 guidebook to London describes some of the different jobs performed by children on the city's streets.

If we went to Covent Garden Market at about five or six o'clock one morning, we should find many of these boys and girls waiting to purchase their stock in trade. There are the flower-girls, choosing and buying their bunches of flowers and fern-leaves, which they will carry to their homes. Arranging them there, and making them into neat little 'button-holes,' they will sally forth after their meagre meal, to the various railway stations from which the streams of City people are pouring into the streets. The sweet scent of their daintily arranged flowers, and their cry of 'Sweet Violets,' soon bring customers. For busy City people like a flower, to remind them of what is beautiful outside the smoky town. Another early bird is the water-cress girl. She goes to market for the fresh young water-cress that is brought from the country in the early hours of the morning. Tying them into bunches as she goes along, her cries of 'Water-cree-sue' will sometimes let us know it is time that we, too, were up. The telegraph-boy is a busy, active lad. Watch him as he goes along, carrying important messages. There is no idling, no stopping to play. He strides along, legs and arms moving in active swing, as though he were walking a race.

The road scavenger boy is busily at work all day in the crowded streets of the City, and seems to have a special **providence** protecting him from harm. His daily life is spent continually within a few inches of horses' hooves and cart wheels. He may be seen just in front of the horses, running, with the help of his scraper and brush, on all-fours, in monkey fashion, and, like a monkey, twisting and turning about out of one danger after another.

And who, on a cold, damp, foggy day, when it seems almost impossible to keep warm, has not enjoyed some of the really hot chestnuts from the tray above the glowing fire of the young chestnut-vendors. With each hand full, we feel the warmth creeping right through us again.

The newspaper boy is, I suppose, considered to be quite as much needed as any of them. We want to know what is happening in the world; what our leading men have to tell us; where our soldiers and sailors are; what is going on in the cold north; and, indeed, we want to know a bit of everything. We travel by 'bus or train, and must read as we go. We have to wait at a station, and must hunt up the news there; and we read out the news as we warm ourselves before the fire at Ionic. These boys know that, and as quickly as they can get away from the publishing office are in the street with piles of papers over their shoulders, and the placard spread out before them, shouting: 'Here y'are, Sir! Special!' With so many papers bringing out several editions during the day, and people so eager for news, there is employment for hundreds of boys. I saw a lad the other day who one night sold a paper to a gentleman, and gave the change for what he, and the gentleman too, thought was a Sixpence. The boy, in counting his money soon afterwards, found that this was a half-sovereign. He was poor, and ten shillings was a mine of wealth to him. It was a great temptation to him to keep it; but I am glad to say he wrapped it in the corner of his handkerchief and returned it to the gentleman when he purchased a paper the next evening. I don't think he sells papers now, for I believe the gentleman got him a situation because of his honesty.

But there are those who find their busiest time when you are asleep. Of these our artist pictures two. The little match-seller, with ragged clothes and with his bare little feet pattering along at our sides, begs us in piteous tones to buy 'a box o' matches, Sir: two hundred and fifty wax-uns for a penny!' 'or two boxes of flamers, the best a-goin'.' And the little orange-girl is sure to be seen quite late at night, standing outside the places of amusement, and offering her 'sweet oranges; three a penny, sweet oranges!'

Not all these lads and lasses are good. Many of them see so much vice at home, and live amid such wicked surroundings, that the wonder is they can be honest at all. But these industries help to make them honest, and keep most of them from a life of crime. And good men and women are at work in and around their homes, and are trying to make them really good. Let us try to help them a little, if we can!

providence care

Extract from *Alton Locke* by Charles Kingsley

FICTION

> The following extract is taken from the novel *Alton Locke*, first published in 1850. Here, Alton begins work as a tailor-boy in the attic of a tailor's shop.

I stumbled after Mr. Jones up a dark, narrow, iron staircase till we emerged through a trap-door into a **garret** at the top of the house. I recoiled with disgust at the scene before me; and here I was to work—perhaps through life! A low lean-to room, stifling me with the combined odours of human breath and perspiration, stale beer, the sweet sickly smell of gin, and the sour and hardly less disgusting one of new cloth. On the floor, thick with dust and dirt, scraps of stuff and ends of thread, sat some dozen haggard, untidy, shoeless men, with a mingled look of care and recklessness that made me shudder. The windows were tight closed to keep out the cold winter air; and the condensed breath ran in streams down the panes, chequering the dreary outlook of chimney-tops and smoke. The conductor handed me over to one of the men.

"Here, Crossthwaite, take this **younker** and make a tailor of him. Keep him next you, and prick him up with your needle if he shirks."

He disappeared down the trap-door, and mechanically, as if in a dream, I sat down by the man and listened to his instructions, kindly enough bestowed. But I did not remain in peace two minutes. A burst of chatter rose as the foreman vanished, and a tall, bloated, sharp-nosed young man next me bawled in my ear,—

"I say, young'un, do you know why we're nearer heaven here than our neighbours?"

"I shouldn't have thought so," answered I with a *naïveté* which raised a laugh, and dashed the tall man for a moment.

"Yer don't? then I'll tell yer. A cause we're a top of the house in the first place, and next place yer'll die here six months sooner nor if yer worked in the room below."

"Why?" asked I.

"A cause you get all the other floors' stinks up here as well as your own. Concentrated essence of man's flesh, is this here as you're a breathing. Cellar workroom we calls Rheumatic Ward, because of the damp. Ground-floor's Fever Ward—them as don't get typhus gets dysentery, and them as don't get dysentery gets typhus—your nose'd tell yer why if you opened the back windy. First floor's Ashmy Ward—don't you hear 'um now through the cracks in the boards, a puffing away like a nest of

THE WORLD OF WORK

young locomotives? And this here most august and upper-crust cockloft is the Conscrumptive Hospital. First you begins to cough,

"Then your cheeks they grows red, and your nose it grows thin,

And your bones they stick out, till they comes through your skin:

"and then, when you've sufficiently covered the poor dear shivering bare backs of the hairystocracy—

"Die, die, die, Away you fly,

Your soul is in the sky!"

And the **ribald** lay down on his back, stretched himself out, and pretended to die in a fit of coughing, which last was, alas! no counterfeit, while poor I, shocked and bewildered, let my tears fall fast upon my knees.

---

garret an attic room
younker child
ribald a person who indulges in vulgar humour

Extract from *Agnes Grey* by Anne Brontë

In the Victorian era, one of the few jobs open to educated women was to work as a governess teaching the children of wealthy families. In this extract from the novel *Agnes Grey*, which first published in 1847, Agnes has been employed as a governess by the Bloomfield family and here Mrs Bloomfield introduces Agnes to the children she will teaching.

Master Tom Bloomfield was a well-grown boy of seven, with a somewhat wiry frame, flaxen hair, blue eyes, small turned-up nose, and fair complexion. Mary Ann was a tall girl too, somewhat dark like her mother, but with a round full face and a high colour in her cheeks. The second sister was Fanny, a very pretty little girl; Mrs. Bloomfield assured me she was a remarkably gentle child, and required encouragement: she had not learned anything yet; but in a few days, she would be four years old, and then she might take her first lesson in the alphabet, and be promoted to the schoolroom. The remaining one was Harriet, a little broad, fat, merry, playful thing of scarcely two, that I coveted more than all the rest—but with her I had nothing to do.

I talked to my little pupils as well as I could, and tried to render myself agreeable; but with little success I fear, for their mother's presence kept me under an unpleasant restraint. They, however, were remarkably free from shyness. They seemed bold, lively children, and I hoped I should soon be on friendly terms with them—the little boy especially, of whom I had heard such a favourable character from his mamma. In Mary Ann there was a certain affected simper, and a craving for notice, that I was sorry to observe. But her brother claimed all my attention to himself; he stood bolt upright between me and the fire, with his hands behind his back, talking away like an orator, occasionally interrupting his discourse with a sharp reproof to his sisters when they made too much noise.

"Oh, Tom, what a darling you are!" exclaimed his mother. "Come and kiss dear mamma; and then won't you show Miss Grey your schoolroom, and your nice new books?"

"I won't kiss *you*, mamma; but I *will* show Miss Grey my schoolroom, and my new books."

"And *my* schoolroom, and *my* new books, Tom," said Mary Ann. "They're mine too."

"They're *mine*," replied he decisively. "Come along, Miss Grey—I'll escort you."

When the room and books had been shown, with some bickerings between the brother and sister that I did my utmost to appease or mitigate, Mary Ann brought me her doll, and began to be very **loquacious** on the subject of its fine clothes, its bed, its chest of drawers, and other **appurtenances**; but Tom told her to hold her clamour, that Miss Grey might see his rocking-horse, which, with a most important bustle, he dragged forth from its corner into the middle of the room, loudly calling on me to attend to it. Then, ordering his sister to hold the reins, he mounted, and made me stand for ten minutes, watching how manfully he used his whip and spurs. Meantime, however, I admired Mary Ann's pretty doll, and all its possessions; and then told Master Tom he was a capital rider, but I hoped he would not use his whip and spurs so much when he rode a real pony.

"Oh, yes, I will!" said he, laying on with redoubled **ardour**. "I'll cut into him like smoke! Eeh! my word! but he shall sweat for it."

This was very shocking; but I hoped in time to be able to work a **reformation**.

"Now you must put on your bonnet and shawl," said the little hero, "and I'll show you my garden."

"And *mine*," said Mary Ann.

Tom lifted his fist with a menacing gesture; she uttered a loud, shrill scream, ran to the other side of me, and made a face at him.

"Surely, Tom, you would not strike your sister! I hope I shall *never* see you do that."

"You will sometimes: I'm obliged to do it now and then to keep her in order."

"But it is not your business to keep her in order, you know—that is for—"

"Well, now go and put on your bonnet."

"I don't know—it is so very cloudy and cold, it seems likely to rain;—and you know I have had a long drive."

"No matter—you *must* come; I shall allow of no excuses," replied the consequential little gentleman. And, as it was the first day of our acquaintance, I thought I might as well indulge him. It was too cold for Mary Ann to venture, so she stayed with her mamma, to the great relief of her brother, who liked to have me all to himself.

The garden was a large one, and tastefully laid out; besides several splendid dahlias, there were some other fine flowers still in bloom: but my companion would not give me time to examine them: I must go with him, across the wet grass, to a remote sequestered corner, the most important place in the grounds, because it contained *his* garden. There were two round beds, stocked with a variety of plants. In one there was a pretty little rose-tree. I paused to admire its lovely blossoms.

"Oh, never mind that!" said he, contemptuously. "That's only *Mary Ann's* garden; look, THIS is mine."

After I had observed every flower, and listened to a disquisition on every plant, I was permitted to depart;

but first, with great pomp, he plucked a **polyanthus** and presented it to me, as one conferring a prodigious favour. I observed, on the grass about his garden, certain apparatus of sticks and corn, and asked what they were.

"Traps for birds."

"Why do you catch them?"

"Papa says they do harm."

"And what do you do with them when you catch them?"

"Different things. Sometimes I give them to the cat."

---

loquacious talkative
appurtenances equipment
ardour fervour
reformation the act of reforming somebody
polyanthus a type of flower

Extract from a magazine article in *The Girl's Own Paper*

> The following extract is taken from a magazine article published in *The Girl's Own Paper* on 2nd December 1899. Here, the author presents her views on young women and the jobs they can do.

During the last few years it has been the fashion for people of all sorts and conditions to busy themselves about us and our position; they have given their opinions of us very freely, they have discussed our capabilities, or rather incapabilities, together with our future prospects very much as though we were **marionettes**, without souls or brains or hands.

If any among us are idle, and a good many of us are credited with this disease, we are rebuked; if, on the contrary, we are industrious and earn an independent livelihood, we are abused for taking the bread out of our brothers' mouths.

If we do not work, we are told that we cannot make good wives; and if we do work, that we shall be unable to make our husbands happy because they want companions more or less frivolous when they have been at work all day. Alas! we should be thoroughly deserving of all the compassion showered upon us from time to time, if we were moved one iota from our steady purposes by all the conflicting advice and opinions offered us.

It is our determination not to be objects of compassion, neither will we be useless **lumber** in our homes, neither will we arrange our lives with the one purpose of entrapping men to marry us.

Are we to be sorry that it is now quite rare to find, among us girls, one that sits down all day reading novels with a pet dog in her lap which she from time to time caresses, or that a girl willing to work is deterred from it by the fear of lowering her position thereby?

We are convinced that work is good for us; we are better for it physically, mentally and spiritually. We are altogether happier for it, and we object to being **compassionated** for doing that which our talents fit us for.

No girl will be the worse for a little money in the Savings Bank, but it will go doubly as far as if she has placed it there out of her own earnings and not out of her father's.

We look round upon many families we know, and wherever we see a girl petted and thought too pretty or too delicate or too anything else to work, she is invariably discontented and unhappy - and why? Because she is not fulfilling her mission in the world.

If, as people say, we are robbing our brothers of their work, it must be because we take more pains with the work and do it better than they. Therefore let them look to it.

There is work for everybody; if not in one way, then in another. A lady whom some of us know was once very rich, and when her husband died she found herself quite poor, and would have been obliged to live upon her friends but for one gift she possessed, and peculiar as it was, she resolved to use it. It was that of mending clothes and linen, which she could do beautifully. She made her position known to several families who gladly engaged her on stated days of the month from nine in the morning till six in the evening, and needless to say, she is proving the greatest comfort possible to mothers of large families. For some years now she has kept herself not only independent, but able to put by a little for old age or sickness, and no one thinks of looking down upon her because she is doing the one thing she knows she could do well.

In the same way a clergyman's daughter deprived of means had to face the world for herself and little sister, and knew that no one could clean or trim lamps better than she. So she at once made this accomplishment known, and she is getting a very tolerable income in this way without any loss of self-respect.

Working does not make us less womanly or less helpful in our homes or less affectionate to our parents, or, depend upon it, God would not have given us the capacity and the ability to work.

Who is the strength and the brightness of the home - the busy or the idle girl? The one who uses her brains or the one who lets them rust?

If people will interfere with us at all, let them try to build us up in vigorous, healthful work, teaching us that however humble the work we do, we give it dignity by doing it to the best of our ability.

We have come to the conclusion that we shall live better lives and longer lives if we work well and cheerfully at that which falls to our lot. The nation will be the better for our influence and example, and our brothers cannot and will not be content to smoke and dawdle away their time at clubs and music halls while we, their sisters, are earnestly working.

At the same time we will endeavour to hold fast by those attributes of modesty, gentleness and patience which belong to good women, and while we enrich the home with our earnings, we will try to be its sunlight and its ornament.

---

marionette a puppet on strings
lumber something useless
compassionated showing compassion to

Rich and poor

In the 19th century a stark contrast could be seen between the lives of the rich and the lives of the poor. As the Industrial Revolution drove people to towns and cities in search of work, poor families crowded together in slums, with several families sometimes living together in a single room, whilst wealthy families lived in large, comfortable houses staffed by servants.

The children of the poor were often forced onto the streets to earn a living for their families, working as road-sweepers, flower-sellers or performing other menial jobs, whilst others turned to a life of crime. Workhouses provided shelter and employment for the destitute, but the harsh conditions found in these places meant that many instead lived homeless on the streets.

At this time, the issue of poverty became a matter of national debate. Some people blamed the poor for being agents of their own misfortune, but other prominent figures, the author Charles Dickens amongst them, tried to help the impoverished with charities established to bring aid to those in need.

Extract from *The Water-Babies* by Charles Kingsley

> In this extract from the novel *The Water-Babies*, which was first published in 1863, a young chimney-sweep called Tom becomes lost whilst cleaning the chimneys of a grand house and finds himself in a young girl's bedroom.

How many chimneys Tom swept I cannot say; but he swept so many that he got quite tired, and puzzled too, for they were not like the town flues to which he was accustomed, but such as you would find—if you would only get up them and look, which perhaps you would not like to do—in old country-houses, large and crooked chimneys, which had been altered again and again, till they ran one into another, **anastomosing** (as Professor Owen would say) considerably. So Tom fairly lost his way in them; not that he cared much for that, though he was in pitchy darkness, for he was as much at home in a chimney as a mole is underground; but at last, coming down as he thought the right chimney, he came down the wrong one, and found himself standing on the hearthrug in a room the like of which he had never seen before.

Tom had never seen the like. He had never been in gentlefolks' rooms but when the carpets were all up, and the curtains down, and the furniture huddled together under a cloth, and the pictures covered with aprons and dusters; and he had often enough wondered what the rooms were like when they were all ready for the quality to sit in. And now he saw, and he thought the sight very pretty.

The room was all dressed in white,—white window-curtains, white bed-curtains, white furniture, and white walls, with just a few lines of pink here and there. The carpet was all over gay little flowers; and the walls were hung with pictures in gilt frames, which amused Tom very much. There were pictures of ladies and gentlemen, and pictures of horses and dogs. The horses he liked; but the dogs he did not care for much, for there were no bull-dogs among them, not even a terrier. But the two pictures which took his fancy most were, one a man in long garments, with little children and their mothers round him, who was laying his hand upon the children's heads. That was a very pretty picture, Tom thought, to hang in a lady's room. For he could see that it was a lady's room by the dresses which lay about.

The other picture was that of a man nailed to a cross, which surprised Tom much. He fancied that he had seen something like it in a shop-window. […]

The next thing he saw, and that too puzzled him, was a washing-stand, with ewers and basins, and soap and brushes, and towels, and a large bath full of clean water—what a heap of things all for washing! "She must be a very dirty lady," thought Tom, "by my master's rule, to want as much scrubbing as all that. But she must be very cunning to put the dirt out of the way so well afterwards, for I don't see a speck about the room, not even on the very towels."

And then, looking toward the bed, he saw that dirty lady, and held his breath with astonishment.

Under the snow-white coverlet, upon the snow-white pillow, lay the most beautiful little girl that Tom had ever seen. Her cheeks were almost as white as the pillow, and her hair was like threads of gold spread all about over the bed. She might have been as old as Tom, or maybe a year or two older; but Tom did not think of that. He thought only of her delicate skin and golden hair, and wondered whether she was a real live person, or one of the wax dolls he had seen in the shops. But when he saw her breathe, he made up his mind that she was alive, and stood staring at her, as if she had been an angel out of heaven.

No. She cannot be dirty. She never could have been dirty, thought Tom to himself. And then he thought, "And are all people like that when they are washed?" And he looked at his own wrist, and tried to rub the soot off, and wondered whether it ever would come off. "Certainly I should look much prettier then, if I grew at all like her."

And looking round, he suddenly saw, standing close to him, a little ugly, black, ragged figure, with bleared eyes and grinning white teeth. He turned on it angrily. And behold, it was himself, reflected in a great mirror, the like of which Tom had never seen before.

And Tom, for the first time in his life, found out that he was dirty; and burst into tears with shame and anger; and turned to sneak up the chimney again and hide; and upset the fender and threw the fire-irons down, with a noise as of ten thousand tin kettles tied to ten thousand mad dogs' tails.

Up jumped the little white lady in her bed, and, seeing Tom, screamed as shrill as any peacock. In rushed a stout old nurse from the next room, and seeing Tom likewise, made up her mind that he had come to rob, plunder, destroy, and burn; and dashed at him, as he lay over the fender, so fast that she caught him by the jacket.

But she did not hold him. Tom had been in a policeman's hands many a time, and out of them too, what is more; and he would have been ashamed to face his friends for ever if he had been stupid enough to be caught by an old woman; so he doubled under the good lady's arm, across the room, and out of the window in a moment.

---

anastomosing connecting (a medical term that refers to blood vessels or veins)

Article from *London Labour and the London Poor*

The journalist Henry Mayhew wrote a series of articles about the lives of the poor in Victorian London. In this article, published in *London Labour and the London Poor* in 1851, he interviews a young girl who sells bundles of watercress on the street to make money for her family.

The poor child, although the weather was severe, was dressed in a thin cotton gown, with a threadbare shawl wrapped round her shoulders. She wore no covering to her head, and the long rusty hair stood out in all directions. When she walked she shuffled along, for fear that the large carpet slippers that served her for shoes should slip off her feet.

"I go about the streets with **water-creases**, crying, 'Four bunches a penny, water-creases.' I am just eight years old - that's all, and I've a big sister, and a brother and a sister younger than I am. On and off, I've been very near a twelvemonth in the streets. My mother learned me to needle-work and to knit when I was about five. I used to go to school, too; but I wasn't there long. I've forgot all about it now, it's such a time ago; and mother took me away because the master whacked me. I didn't like him at all. What do you think? He hit me three times, ever so hard, across the face with his cane, and made me go dancing down stairs.

The **creases** is so bad now, that I haven't been out with 'em for three days. They're so cold, people won't buy 'em; for when I goes up to them, they say, 'They'll freeze our bellies.' In summer there's lots, and 'most as cheap as dirt; but I have to be down at Farringdon-market between four and five, or else I can't get any creases, because everyone is selling them, and they're picked up so quick. Some of the saleswomen - we never calls 'em ladies – is very kind to us children, and some of them altogether spiteful. I used to go down to market along with another girl, as must be about fourteen, 'cos she does her back hair up. When we've bought a lot, we sits down on a door-step, and ties up the bunches. We never goes home to breakfast till we've sold out; but, if it's very late, then I buys a penn'orth of **pudden**, which is very nice with gravy.

It's very cold before winter comes on reg'lar - specially getting up of a morning. I gets up in the dark by the light of the lamp in the court. When the snow is on the ground, there's no creases. I bears the cold - you must; so I puts my hands under my shawl, though it hurts 'em to take hold of the creases, especially when we takes 'em to the pump to wash 'em. No; I never see any children crying - it's no use.

81

Sometimes I make a great deal of money. One day I took one shilling six pence, and the creases cost six pence; but it isn't often I get such luck as that. I oftener makes three pence or four pence than one shilling; and then I'm at work, crying, 'Creases, four bunches a penny, creases!' from six in the morning to about ten.

I always give mother my money, she's so very good to me. She don't often beat me; but, when she do, she don't play with me. She's very poor, and goes out cleaning rooms sometimes, now she don't work at the fur. I ain't got no father, he's a father-in-law. No; mother ain't married again – he's a father-in-law. He grinds scissors, and he's very good to me. No; I dont mean by that that he says kind things to me, for he never hardly speaks. When I gets home, after selling creases, I stops at home. I puts the room to rights: mother don't make me do it, I does it myself. I cleans the chairs, though there's only two to clean. I takes a tub and scrubbing-brush and flannel, and scrubs the floor - that's what I do three or four times a week."

---

water-creases, creases watercress
pudden a sweet dessert

Extract from *Paved with Gold* by Augustus Mayhew

FICTION

> The following extract is taken from the novel *Paved With Gold*, which was first published in 1858. Augustus Mayhew was Henry Mayhew's brother and this novel drew on his knowledge of the lives of London's poor, which he gained from helping his brother. Here, he describes a crowd of people waiting for a homeless refuge to open.

It is impossible to mistake the asylum if you go there at dark, just as the lamp in the wire cage over the entrance-door is being lighted; for this is the hour for opening, and ranged along the kerb is a kind of ragged regiment, drawn up four deep, and stretching far up and down the narrow lane, until the crowd is like a hedge to the roadway.

Nowhere in the world can a similar sight be witnessed.

It is a terrible thing to look down upon that squalid crowd from one of the upper windows. There they stand shivering in the snow, with their thin cobwebby garments hanging in tatters about them. Many are without shirts; with their bare skin showing through the rents and gaps, like the hide of a dog with the mange. Some have their greasy garments tied round their wrists and ankles with string, to prevent the piercing wind from blowing up them. A few are without shoes, and these keep one foot only to the ground, while the bare flesh that has had to tramp through the snow is blue and livid-looking, as half-cooked meat.

You can pick out the different foreigners and countrymen in that wretched throng by the different colours of their costume. There you see the black sailor in his faded red woollen shirt; the **Lascar** in his dirty-white calico tunic; the Frenchman in his short blue smock; the countryman in his clay-stained frock, with the bosom worked all over like a dirty sampler; and the Irish market-woman with her faded straw bonnet, flattened by the heavy loads she has borne on her head.

The mob is of all ages, and women and girls as well as men and boys are huddled there close together. There are old-looking lads, shrinking within their clothes with the cold, and blowing their nails to warm their finger-tips; and mothers with their bosoms bare, despite the keenness of the weather, and the beggar babes sucking vainly at them. Each man has his hands in his pockets, and every now and then he shudders rather than shivers, as if positively palsied by the frost, whilst the women have the ends of their thin shawls and gauzy **mantles** rolled round their bare arms, like the cloths about a **brigand**'s legs.

It is a sullenly silent crowd, without any of the riot and **rude** frolic which generally ensues upon any gathering in the London streets; for the only sounds heard are the squealing of the beggar infants, or the wrangling of the vagrant boys for the front ranks, together with a continued Succession of hoarse coughs, that seem to answer each other like the bleating of a flock of sheep.

Poor souls! they are waiting in the numbing cold for those barn-like doors to open, and as the time draws near, those in the front are seen unfolding the bit of old rag or dirty paper in which they have secured the ticket that entitles them to some one or two nights' further shelter.

It was to this refuge that the policeman referred when he said to the woman whom he found half frozen on the door-step, "The asylum for the houseless is the only place for you." It was to this refuge that the officer and the faint and weary creature were on their way - so faint and weary, indeed, that Heaven only knows what wretched fate would befall her if the bare hospitality of the place should be denied to her.

Lascar an Indian sailor
mantle cloak
brigand robber
rude unpleasantly forceful

Extract from *Jan of the Windmill* by Juliana Horatio Ewing

FICTION

> The following extract is taken from the novel *Jan of the Windmill*, first published in 1876. Here, a young boy called Jan is working as a street artist to earn money for his master, Cheap Jack.

There was a large crowd, but large crowds gather quickly in London from small causes. It was in an out-of-the-way spot too, and the police had not yet tried to disperse it.

The crowd was gathered round a street-artist who was "screeving," or drawing pictures on the pavement in colored chalks. A good many men have followed the trade in London with some success, but this artist was a wan, meagre-looking child. It was Jan. He drew with extraordinary rapidity; not with the rapidity of slovenliness, but with the rapidity of a genius in the choice of what **Ruskin** calls "fateful lines." At his back stood the hunchback, who "pattered" in description of the drawings as glibly as he used to "**puff**" his own wares as a Cheap Jack.

"Cats on the roof of a 'ouse. Look at 'em, ladies and gentlemen; and from their harched backs to their tails and whiskers, and the moon a-shining in the sky, you'll say they're as natteral as life. Bo-serve the fierceness in the eye of that black Tom. The one that's a-coming round the chimney-pot is a Sandy; yellow ochre in the body, and the markings in red. There isn't a harpist living could do 'em better, though I says it that's the lad's father."

The cats were very popular, and so were the Prize Pig, Playful Porkers, Sow and her Little Ones, as exhibited by the Cheap Jack. But the prime favorite was "The Faithful Friend," consisting of sketches of Rufus in various **attitudes**, including a last sleep on the grave of a **supposititious** master, which Jan drew with a heart that ached as if it must break.

It was growing dark, but the exhibition had been so successful that day, and the crowd was still so large, that the hunchback was loath to desist. At a sign from him, Jan put his colored chalks into a little pouch in front of him, and drew in powerful chiaroscuro with soft black chalk and whitening. These sketches were visible for some time, and the interest of the crowd did not abate.

Suddenly a flush came over Jan's wan cheeks. A baker who had paused for a moment to look, and then passed on, was singing as he went, and the song and the man's accent were both familiar to Jan.

"The swallow twitters on the barn,
The rook is cawing on the tree,

And in the wood the ring-dove coos" –

"What's your name, boy?"

The **peremptory** tone of the question turned Jan's attention from the song, which died away down the street, and looking up he met a pair of eyes as black as his own, and Mr. Ford's client repeated his question. On seeing that a "**swell**" had paused to look, the Cheap Jack hurried to Jan's side, and was in time to answer.

"John Smith's his name, sir. He's slow of speech, my lord, though very quick with his pencil. There's not many artists can beat him, though I says it that shouldn't, being his father."

"*You* his father?" said the gentleman. "He is not much like you."

"He favours his mother more, my lord," said the Cheap Jack; "and that's where he gets his talents too."

"No one ever thought he got 'em from you, old hump!" said one of the spectators, and there was a roar of laughter from the bystanders.

Mr. Ford's client still lingered, though the staring and pushing of the rude crowd were annoying to him.

"Do you really belong to this man?" he asked of Jan, and Jan replied, trembling, "Yes, sir."

"Your son doesn't look as if you treated him very well," said the gentleman, turning to the Cheap Jack. "Take that, and give him a good supper this evening. He deserves it."

As the Cheap Jack stooped for the half crown thrown to him, Mr. Ford's client gave Jan some pence, saying, "You can keep these yourself." Jan's face, with a look of gratitude upon it, seemed to startle him afresh, but it was getting dark, and the crowd was closing round him. Jan had just entertained a wild thought of asking his protection, when he was gone.

What the strange gentleman had said about his unlikeness to the Cheap Jack, and also the thoughts awakened by hearing the old song, gave new energy to a resolve to which Jan had previously come. He had resolved to run away.

Ruskin John Ruskin, a leading Victorian art critic
puff promote
attitudes poses
supposititious substituted for the real thing
peremptory authoritative
swell a rich person

Extract from the diary of Arthur Munby

> This extract is taken from the diary of Arthur Munby, an amateur artist who lived in London. In this entry, written in 1864, he describes the beggars he encounters in St. James's Park.

Friday, 15 July

Walking through St. James's Park about 4 p.m., I found the open spaces of **sward** on either side the path thickly dotted over with strange dark objects. They were human beings; ragged men & ragged women; lying prone & motionless, not as those who lie down for rest & enjoyment, but as creatures worn out and listless. A park keeper came up: who are these? I asked. They are men out of work, said he, and unfortunate girls; servant girls, many of them, what has been out of place and took to the streets, till they've sunk so low that they can't get a living. It's like this every day, till winter comes; and then what they do I don't know. They come as soon as the gates opens; always the same faces: they bring broken victuals with 'em, or else goes to the soup kitchen in Vinegar Yard;

and except for that, they lie about here all day. It's a disgrace Sir (said he), to go on in a City like this; and foreigners to see it, too! Why Sir, these unfortunates are all over the place: the ground (he added with a gesture of disgust) is lousy with them'. I looked and looked and still they did not move. The men were more or less tattered, but their dress was working dress, & so did not seem out of place. But the girls were clothed in what had once been finery: filthy draggled **muslins**; thin remnants of shawls, all rent and gaping; crushed and greasy bonnets of fashionable shape, with sprigs of torn flowers, bits of faded velvet, hanging from them. Their hands and faces were dirty & weather-stained; and they lay, not (as far I saw) herding with the men, but singly or in little groups; sprawling about the grass in attitudes ungainly, and unfeminine, and bestial: one flat on her face, another curled up like a dog with her head between her knees; another with her knees bent under her, and her cheek on the ground, and her arms spread out stiff and awkward, on either side of her. Every pose expressed an absolute degradation and despair: and the silence & deadness of the **prostrate** crowd was appalling. I counted these as I went along; and on one side only of one path (leading from the lake to the Mall), there were one hundred and five of them. 105 forlorn and **foetid** outcasts - women, many of them - grovelling on the sward, in the bright sunshine of a July afternoon, with Carlton House Terrace and Westminster Abbey looking down at them, and infinite **well-drest** citizens passing by on the other side.

sward lawn
muslins cotton
prostrate lying down
foetid foul-smelling
well-drest well-dressed

Extract from the essay *How the Poor Live* by George Sims

> The following extract is taken from *How the Poor Live*, an essay written by the journalist George Sims and published in 1883. Here, the author describes in a humorous way a typical room rented by a poor family.

One room in this district is very like the other. The family likeness of the chairs and tables is truly remarkable, especially in the matter of legs. Most chairs are born with four legs, but the chairs one meets with here are a two-legged race – a four-legged chair is a *rara avis*, and when found should be made a note of. The tables, too, are of a type **indigenous** to the spot. The survival of the fittest does not obtain in these districts in the matter of tables. The most positively unfit are common, very common objects. What has become of the fittest I hesitate to **conjecture**. Possibly they have run away. I am quite sure that a table with legs would make use of them to escape from such surroundings.

As to the bedsteads, they are wretched, broken-down

old things of wood and iron that look as though they had been rescued a little late from a fire, then used for a barricade, afterwards buried in volcanic eruption, and finally dug out of a dust-heap that had concealed them for a century. The bedding, a respectable coal-sack would blush to acknowledge even as a poor relation.

The 'furnished apartments' fetch as much as tenpence a day, and are sometimes occupied by three or four different tenants during a week.

The 'deputy' comes for the money every day, and it is pay or go with the occupants. If the man who has taken one of these furnished rooms for his 'home, sweet home' does not get enough during the day to pay his rent, out he goes into the street with his wife and children, and enter another family **forthwith**.

The tenants have not, as a rule, much to be flung after them in the shape of goods and **chattels**. The clothes they stand uptight in, a battered kettle, and, perhaps, a bundle, make up the catalogue of their worldly possessions.

---

rara avis a rare person or thing
indigenous particular to a certain area
conjecture guess
forthwith immediately
chattels belongings

Extract from *The Condition of the Working Class in England* by Friedrich Engels

> This extract is taken from *The Condition of the Working Class* in England. The book was written during Friedrich Engels' stay in Manchester from 1842 to 1844 and first published in English in 1887. Here, he describes the slum housing in the city at this time.

In a rather deep hole, in a curve of the **Medlock** and surrounded on all four sides by tall factories and high embankments, covered with buildings, stand two groups of about two hundred cottages, built chiefly back to back, in which live about four thousand human beings, most of them Irish. The cottages are old, dirty, and of the smallest sort, the streets uneven, fallen into ruts and in part without drains or pavement; masses of refuse, offal and sickening filth lie among standing pools in all directions; the atmosphere is poisoned by the **effluvia** from these, and laden and darkened by the smoke of a dozen tall factory chimneys. A horde of ragged women and children swarm about here, as filthy as the swine that thrive upon the garbage heaps and in the puddles. In short, the whole **rookery** furnishes such a hateful and repulsive spectacle as can hardly be equalled in the worst court on the **Irk**. The race that lives in these ruinous cottages, behind broken windows, mended with oilskin, sprung doors, and rotten door-posts, or in dark, wet cellars, in measureless filth and stench, in this atmosphere penned in as if with a purpose, this race must really have reached the lowest stage of humanity. This is the impression and the line of thought which the exterior of this district forces upon the beholder. But what must one think when he hears that in each of these pens, containing at most two rooms, a garret and perhaps a cellar, on the average twenty human beings live.

On Monday, Jan. 15th, 1844, two boys were brought before the police magistrate because, being in a starving condition, they had stolen and immediately devoured a half-cooked calf's foot from a shop. The magistrate felt called upon to investigate the case further, and received the following details from the policeman: The mother of the two boys was the widow of an ex-soldier, afterwards policeman, and had had a very hard time since the death of her husband, to provide for her nine children. She lived at No. 2 Pool's Place, Quaker Court, Spitalfields, in the utmost poverty. When the policeman came to her, he found her with six of her children literally huddled together in a little back room, with no furniture but two old rush-bottomed chairs with the seats gone, a small table with two legs broken, a broken cup, and a small dish. On the hearth was scarcely a spark of fire, and in one corner lay as many old rags as would fill a woman's apron, which served the whole family as a bed. For bed clothing they had only their scanty day clothing. The poor woman told him that she had been forced to sell her bedstead the year before to buy food. Her bedding she had pawned with the victualler for food. In short, everything had gone for food.

Medlock a river in Manchester
effluvia fumes given off by waste
rookery slum
Irk a river in Manchester

Extract from *A Plea for Ragged Schools* by Thomas Guthrie

The following extract is taken from *A Plea for Ragged Schools*, first published in 1847. Here, Thomas Guthrie describes seeing homeless children seeking shelter for the night in a police station.

The Night Asylum was not then established; but the houseless, the inhabitants of arches and stair-foots found, when they sought it, or dared to seek it, a shelter in the Police Office. I had often heard of the misery it presented; and, detained at a meeting till past midnight, I went with one of my elders, who was a Commissioner of Police, to visit the scene. In a room, the walls of which were thickly hung with bunches of skeleton keys, the dark lanterns of the thief, and other instruments of housebreaking, sat the lieutenant of the watch. Seeing me at that untimely hour, handed in by one of the Commissioners, he looked surprise itself. Having satisfied him that there was no misdemeanour, we proceeded, under the charge of an intelligent officer, to visit the **wards**.

Our purpose is not to describe the strangest, saddest collection of human misery I ever saw, but to observe that not a few children, having no home on earth, had sought and found there a shelter for the night. "They had not where to lay their head." Turned adrift in the morning, and subsisting as they best could during the day, this wreck of society, like the **wrack** of the sea-shore, came drifting in again at evening tide. After visiting a number of wards and cells, I remember looking down from the gallery on an open space, where five or six human beings lay on the bare pavement buried in slumber; and right opposite the stove, with its ruddy light shining full on his face, lay a poor child, who attracted my special attention. He was miserably clad; he seemed about eight years old; he had the sweetest face I ever saw; his bed was the hard stone pavement, – his pillow a brick; and, as he lay calm in sleep, forgetful of all his sorrows, he looked a picture of injured innocence. His story, which I learned from the officer, was a sad one; but one such as too many could tell. He had neither father nor mother, brother nor friend, in the wide world. His only friends were the Police, – his only home their office. How he lived they did not know; but, sent away in the morning, he usually returned at night. The floor of a ward, the stone by the stove, was a better bed than a stair-foot. I could not get that boy out of my head or heart for days and nights together.

---

wards rooms
wrack wreckage

Transport and travel

A revolution in transportation took place in the 19th century. As the century dawned, the horse and carriage was still the main form of transportation, carrying goods and people from place to place. By the century's end, motorcars could be seen on the roads of Great Britain whilst a network of railway lines criss-crossed the country, transforming the time it took to get around.

The streets of Britain's cities became increasingly crowded as the century wore on, with new inventions such as the bicycle jostling for space with horse-drawn hansom cabs and omnibuses. Incidences of road rage were seen and the first traffic lights were introduced in London in 1868, whilst beneath the city streets the first underground trains began running in 1890.

From boats to bicycles, balloons to trains, the 19th century transformed the way in which people travelled for both work and pleasure. Faster forms of transport opened up new horizons and helped make the world feel like a smaller place.

Extract from *Recollections of a Girlhood* by Frances Ann Kemble

> The following extract from Frances Ann Kemble's
> memoir *Recollections of a Girlhood*, first published in 1879,
> gives an eyewitness account of an accident that marred
> the opening of the Liverpool–Manchester Railway on
> 15th September 1830.

"The engine had stopped to take in a supply of water,
and several of the gentlemen in the directors' carriage
had jumped out to look about them. Lord Wilton, Count
Batthyany, Count Matuscenitz, and Mr. Huskisson
among the rest were standing talking in the middle of
the road, when an engine on the other line, which was
parading up and down merely to show its speed, was
seen coming down upon them like lightning. The most
active of those in peril sprang back into their seats; Lord
Wilton saved his life only by rushing behind the Duke's
carriage, and Count Matuscenitz had but just leaped into
it, with the engine all but touching his heels as he did
so; while poor Mr. Huskisson, less active from the effects
of age and ill-health, bewildered, too, by the frantic cries
of 'Stop the engine! Clear the track!' that resounded on

all sides, completely lost his head, looked helplessly to the right and left, and was instantaneously **prostrated** by the fatal machine, which dashed down like a thunderbolt upon him, and passed over his leg, smashing and mangling it in the most horrible way. (Lady Wilton said she distinctly heard the crushing of the bone.) So terrible was the effect of the appalling accident that, except that ghastly 'crushing' and poor Mrs. Huskisson's piercing shriek, not a sound was heard or a word uttered among the immediate spectators of the catastrophe."

---

prostrated laid face down

Extract from *Dombey and Son* by Charles Dickens

This extract is taken from the novel *Dombey and Son*, first published in 1848. Here, Dickens describes a train journey taken by Mr Dombey.

The very speed at which the train was whirled along, mocked the swift course of the young life that had been borne away so steadily and so **inexorably** to its **foredoomed** end. The power that forced itself upon its iron way—its own—defiant of all paths and roads, piercing through the heart of every obstacle, and dragging living creatures of all classes, ages, and degrees behind it, was a type of the triumphant monster, Death.

Away, with a shriek, and a roar, and a rattle, from the town, burrowing among the dwellings of men and making the streets hum, flashing out into the meadows for a moment, mining in through the damp earth, booming on in darkness and heavy air, bursting out again into the sunny day so bright and wide; away, with a shriek, and a roar, and a rattle, through the fields, through the woods, through the corn, through the hay, through the chalk, through the mould, through the clay, through the rock, among objects close at hand and almost in the grasp, ever flying from the traveller, and a deceitful distance ever moving slowly within him: like as in the track of the remorseless monster, Death!

Through the hollow, on the height, by the heath, by the orchard, by the park, by the garden, over the canal, across the river, where the sheep are feeding, where the mill is going, where the barge is floating, where the dead are lying, where the factory is smoking, where the stream is running, where the village clusters, where the great cathedral rises, where the bleak moor lies, and the wild breeze smooths or ruffles it at its inconstant will; away, with a shriek, and a roar, and a rattle, and no trace to leave behind but dust and vapour: like as in the track of the remorseless monster, Death!

Breasting the wind and light, the shower and sunshine, away, and still away, it rolls and roars, fierce and rapid, smooth and certain, and great works and massive bridges crossing up above, fall like a beam of shadow an inch broad, upon the eye, and then are lost. Away, and still away, onward and onward ever: glimpses of cottage-homes, of houses, mansions, rich estates, of **husbandry** and handicraft, of people, of old roads and paths that look deserted, small, and insignificant as they are left behind: and so they do, and what else is there but such glimpses, in the track of the indomitable monster, Death!

Away, with a shriek, and a roar, and a rattle, plunging

down into the earth again, and working on in such a storm of energy and perseverance, that amidst the darkness and whirlwind the motion seems reversed, and to tend furiously backward, until a ray of light upon the wet wall shows its surface flying past like a fierce stream. Away once more into the day, and through the day, with a shrill yell of exultation, roaring, rattling, tearing on, spurning everything with its dark breath, sometimes pausing for a minute where a crowd of faces are, that in a minute more are not; sometimes lapping water greedily, and before the spout at which it drinks has ceased to drip upon the ground, shrieking, roaring, rattling through the purple distance!

Louder and louder yet, it shrieks and cries as it comes tearing on resistless to the goal: and now its way, still like the way of Death, is strewn with ashes thickly.

inexorably relentlessly
foredoomed destined to fail
husbandry farming

Extract from an essay in *Cornhill Magazine* by William Makepeace Thackeray

This extract describing the rapid pace of change brought by the railways is taken from an essay by William Makepeace Thackeray, first published in *Cornhill Magazine* in 1860.

We who have lived before railways were made, belong to another world. In how many hours could the Prince of Wales drive from Brighton to London, with a light carriage built expressly, and relays of horses longing to gallop the next stage? Do you remember Sir Somebody, the coachman of the Age, who took our half-crown so affably? It was only yesterday; but what a gulf between now and then! THEN was the old world. Stage-coaches, more or less swift, riding-horses, pack-horses, highwaymen, knights in armour, Norman invaders, Roman legions, Druids, Ancient Britons painted blue, and so forth--all these belong to the old period.

I will concede a halt in the midst of it, and allow that gunpowder and printing tended to modernize the world. But your railroad starts the new era, and we of a certain age belong to the new time and the old one. We are of the time of chivalry as well as the **Black Prince** or **Sir Walter Manny**. We are of the age of steam. We have stepped out of the old world on to "**Brunel**'s" vast deck, and across the waters. Towards what new continent are we **wending**?

I used to know a man who had invented a flying-machine. "Sir," he would say, "give me but five hundred pounds, and I will make it. It is so simple of construction that I tremble daily lest some other person should light upon and patent my discovery." Perhaps faith was wanting; perhaps the five hundred pounds. He is dead, and somebody else must make the flying-machine. But that will only be a step forward on the journey already begun since we quitted the old world. There it lies on the other side of yonder embankments.

Black Prince a twelfth century prince
Sir Walter Manny a twelfth century soldier
Brunel Isambard Kingdom Brunel, a Victorian civil engineer
who built ships, bridges, railways and tunnels
wending travelling

Extract from *The Wheels of Chance* by H. G. Wells

Towards the end of the 19th century, cycling became increasingly popular as practical and comfortable bicycles became available for the first time. The following extract is taken from the novel *The Wheels of Chance*, first published in 1895, which describes a cycling holiday taken by a young man called Mr Hoopdriver. Here, Mr Hoopdriver sets off through the countryside on his bicycle.

He did not ride fast, he did not ride straight, an exacting critic might say he did not ride well—but he rode generously, **opulently**, using the whole road and even nibbling at the footpath. The excitement never flagged. So far he had never passed or been passed by anything, but as yet the day was young and the road was clear. He doubted his steering so much that, for the present, he had resolved to dismount at the approach of anything else upon wheels. The shadows of the trees lay very long and blue across the road, the morning sunlight was like amber fire.

At the cross-roads at the top of West Hill, where the cattle trough stands, he turned towards Kingston and set himself to scale the little bit of ascent. An early **heath-keeper**, in his velveteen jacket, marvelled at his efforts. And while he yet struggled, the head of a **carter** rose over the brow.

At the sight of him Mr. Hoopdriver, according to his previous determination, resolved to dismount. He tightened the brake, and the machine stopped dead. He was trying to think what he did with his right leg whilst getting off. He gripped the handles and released the brake, standing on the left pedal and waving his right foot in the air. Then—these things take so long in the telling—he found the machine was falling over to the right. While he was deciding upon a plan of action, gravitation appears to have been busy. He was still irresolute when he found the machine on the ground, himself kneeling upon it, and a vague feeling in his mind that again **Providence** had dealt harshly with his shin. This happened when he was just level with the heathkeeper. The man in the approaching cart stood up to see the ruins better.

"THAT ain't the way to get off," said the heathkeeper.

Mr. Hoopdriver picked up the machine. The handle was twisted askew again. He said something under his breath. He would have to unscrew the **beastly** thing.

"THAT ain't the way to get off," repeated the heathkeeper, after a silence.

"*I* know that," said Mr. Hoopdriver, testily, determined to overlook the new specimen on his shin at any cost. He unbuckled the wallet behind the saddle, to get out a screw hammer.

"If you know it ain't the way to get off—whaddyer do it for?" said the heath-keeper, in a tone of friendly controversy.

Mr. Hoopdriver got out his screw hammer and went to the handle. He was annoyed.

"That's my business, I suppose," he said, fumbling with the screw. The unusual exertion had made his hands shake frightfully.

The heath-keeper became meditative, and twisted his stick in his hands behind his back. "You've broken yer 'andle, ain't yer?" he said presently. Just then the screw hammer slipped off the nut. Mr. Hoopdriver used a nasty, low word.

"They're **trying** things, them bicycles," said the heath-keeper, charitably. "Very trying."

Mr. Hoopdriver gave the nut a vicious turn and suddenly stood up—he was holding the front wheel between his knees. "I wish," said he, with a catch in his voice, "I wish you'd leave off staring at me."

Then with the air of one who has delivered an ultimatum, he began replacing the screw hammer in the wallet.

The heath-keeper never moved. Possibly he raised his eyebrows, and certainly he stared harder than he did before. "You're pretty unsociable," he said slowly, as Mr. Hoopdriver seized the handles and stood ready to mount as soon as the cart had passed.

The indignation gathered slowly but surely. "Why don't you ride on a private road of your own if no one ain't to speak to you?" asked the heath-keeper, perceiving more and more clearly the bearing of the matter. "Can't no one make a passin' remark to you, Touchy? Ain't I good enough to speak to you? Been struck wooden all of a sudden?"

---

opulently in an extravagant manner
heath-keeper a person who maintains heathland
carter someone who drives a cart
Providence care
beastly unpleasant
trying difficult

Extract from a magazine article

Cycling became popular amongst women as well as men. The following extract is taken from an article written by Susan, Countess of Malmesbury, and describes her experience of cycling in London. This article was published in *The Badminton Magazine* in 1896.

ON A BICYCLE IN THE STREETS OF LONDON

A new sport has lately been devised by the drivers of **hansom cabs**. It consists of chasing the lady who rides her bicycle in the streets of the metropolis. If not so athletic a pastime as polo, the pursuit on wheels of alien wheels **surmounted** by a **petticoat** which 'half conceals, yet half reveals' the **motive** power within, appears to afford these ingenuous persons exactly that exhilarating and entrancing sensation without which no Englishman finds life worth living, and which apparently is to the heart of the cabby what salmon-fishing, golf, shooting, the rocketting pheasant, hunting the fox, or, in fine, what war, that highest expression of sport, can be to those who are usually called 'the leisured classes.'

I am given to understand that so far the scoring is altogether on the side of the pursuer. He has bagged, we are told, many ladies whose mutilated or decapitated forms have been hurried into silent and secret graves at the instance of the great Bicycle Boom. Their relatives, we hear, have laid them to rest quietly in back gardens until such time as they can **realise** what shares they possess in cycling companies. But whether this be true or not - and, after all, the evening papers must live! - if the harmless necessary Hansom cabman has gained a new pleasure, he has had to pay for it like a prince; for his former attached and confiding fares, instead of **reposing** in the comfortable recesses of his vehicles, are now - stout and thin, short and tall, old and young - all alike vigorously ankle-pedalling just on ahead of his empty and sorrowing cab, and right under the fore-feet of his horse. Small wonder, indeed, if he be jealous and sore.

Having now been the **quarry** of the Hansom cabman for nearly a year, and having given him several exciting runs, I cannot help feeling that cycling in the streets would be nicer, to use a mild expression, if he did not try to kill me; although the pleasure which danger always affords to a certain class of minds would be considerably lessened.

Drivers of hansoms have various ways of inflicting torture on a fellow-creature, one of which is to suddenly and loudly to shout out 'Hi!' when they have ample room to pass, or when you are only occupying your lawful position in a string of vehicles. Also, they love to share your handle-bars and wheels, passing so close that if you swerve in the slightest - which, if you are possessed of nerves, you are likely to do - it must bring you to serious grief. They are also fond of cutting in just in front of you, or deliberately checking you at a crossing, well knowing that by so doing they risk your life, or, at any rate, force you to get off.

I myself always ride peaceably about seven or eight miles an hour, and keep a good look-out some way head, as by that means you can often slip through a tight place or avoid being made into a sandwich composed of, let us say, a pedestrian who will not, and an **omnibus** which cannot, stop.

---

hansom cabs a horse-drawn carriage used as a taxi
surmounted placed above
petticoat a type of underskirt
motive causing motion
realise to be sold for a particular amount of money
reposing resting
quarry prey
omnibus a horse-drawn bus

Extract from *Dracula* by Bram Stoker

> In the following extract from the novel *Dracula*, first published in 1897, Jonathan Harker, a young solicitor from England, is travelling to Castle Dracula in Transylvania to meet his client Count Dracula. Here, he is being taken to the castle at night in a horse-drawn coach.

Soon we were hemmed in with trees, which in places arched right over the roadway till we passed as through a tunnel; and again great frowning rocks guarded us boldly on either side. Though we were in shelter, we could hear the rising wind, for it moaned and whistled through the rocks, and the branches of the trees crashed together as we swept along. It grew colder and colder still, and fine, powdery snow began to fall, so that soon we and all around us were covered with a white blanket. The keen wind still carried the howling of the dogs, though this grew fainter as we went on our way. The baying of the wolves sounded nearer and nearer, as though they were closing round on us from every side. I grew dreadfully afraid, and the horses shared my fear. The driver, however, was not in the least disturbed; he kept turning his head to left and right, but I could not see anything through the darkness.

Suddenly, away on our left, I saw a faint flickering blue flame. The driver saw it at the same moment; he at once checked the horses, and, jumping to the ground, disappeared into the darkness. I did not know what to do, the less as the howling of the wolves grew closer; but while I wondered the driver suddenly appeared again, and without a word took his seat, and we resumed our journey. I think I must have fallen asleep and kept dreaming of the incident, for it seemed to be repeated endlessly, and now looking back, it is like a sort of awful nightmare. Once the flame appeared so near the road, that even in the darkness around us I could watch the driver's motions. He went rapidly to where the blue flame arose—it must have been very faint, for it did not seem to **illumine** the place around it at all—and gathering a few stones, formed them into some device. Once there appeared a strange optical effect: when he stood between me and the flame he did not obstruct it, for I could see its ghostly flicker all the same. This startled me, but as the effect was only momentary, I took it that my eyes deceived me straining through the darkness. Then for a time there were no blue flames, and we sped onwards through the gloom, with the howling of the wolves around us, as though they were following in a moving circle.

At last there came a time when the driver went further

afield than he had yet gone, and during his absence, the horses began to tremble worse than ever and to snort and scream with fright. I could not see any cause for it, for the howling of the wolves had ceased altogether; but just then the moon, sailing through the black clouds, appeared behind the jagged crest of a **beetling**, pine-clad rock, and by its light I saw around us a ring of wolves, with white teeth and lolling red tongues, with long, sinewy limbs and shaggy hair. They were a hundred times more terrible in the grim silence which held them than even when they howled. For myself, I felt a sort of paralysis of fear. It is only when a man feels himself face to face with such horrors that he can understand their true **import**.

All at once the wolves began to howl as though the moonlight had had some peculiar effect on them. The horses jumped about and reared, and looked helplessly round with eyes that rolled in a way painful to see; but the living ring of terror encompassed them on every side; and they had perforce to remain within it. I called to the coachman to come, for it seemed to me that our only chance was to try to break out through the ring and to aid his approach. I shouted and beat the side of the **calèche**, hoping by the noise to scare the wolves from that side, so as to give him a chance of reaching the trap. How he came there, I know not, but I heard his voice raised in a tone of imperious command, and looking towards the sound, saw him stand in the roadway. As he swept his long arms, as though brushing aside some **impalpable** obstacle, the wolves fell back and back further still. Just then a heavy cloud passed across the face of the moon, so that we were again in darkness.

When I could see again the driver was climbing into the calèche, and the wolves had disappeared. This was all so strange and uncanny that a dreadful fear came upon me, and I was afraid to speak or move. The time seemed interminable as we swept on our way, now in almost complete darkness, for the rolling clouds obscured the moon. We kept on ascending, with occasional periods of quick descent, but in the main always ascending. Suddenly, I became conscious of the fact that the driver was in the act of pulling up the horses in the courtyard of a vast ruined castle, from whose tall black windows came no ray of light, and whose broken battlements showed a jagged line against the moonlit sky.

---

illumine light up
beetling overhanging
import meaning
calèche a type of horse-drawn carriage
impalpable imperceptible

Newspaper report

> Road rage is not a modern phenomenon, as this report published in 1838 in the *Morning Post* newspaper shows.

FURIOUS DRIVING

Two stylishly dressed individuals named Stephens and Shreeve, the former of whom stated himself to be a master tailor, were charged under the following circumstances:

It appeared from the evidence of a gentleman named Wilkes, that on the evening before he was walking in the green lanes at Stoke Newington, where his country residence is situated, when he perceived the defendants in a **gig**, which they were driving towards him at a most furious rate, pursued by a policeman on horseback. He had just time to step hastily aside, when the gig passed him so closely that he was within an inch of being run over. The lane was thronged with woman and children, and it appeared almost a miracle that no serious accident occurred.

Police constable 144 N stated that he was on horseback in the lane when the prisoners drove up to him at full speed. He thought the horse had run away at first, but as they passed him the prisoner, Stephens, who was lying on his back, excessively drunk, gave him a cut with his whip. He pursued the gig and after a hard chase, during which Stephens kept incessantly lashing on the horse, he overtook them, and with the assistance of two other policemen, took them into custody. They both resisted and assaulted the officers, and the prisoner Shreeve said that "he would serve them as Lieutenant Bennett had been served."

In their defence the prisoner Shreeve, who acted as spokesman, pleaded his friend's intoxication, and denied that he had used the language **imputed** to him.

Mr. BROUGHTON saizd that it was a most disgraceful transaction, and might have led to fatal consequences.

The prisoner Stephens was ordered to pay a fine of 40 shillings, and the prisoner Shreeve 20 shillings.

gig a type of horse-drawn carriage
imputed attributed

Extract from *Three Men in a Boat* by Jerome K. Jerome

This extract is taken from the novel *Three Men in a Boat*, first published in 1889. This novel describes a boat trip taken by three friends along the river Thames. Here, the friends go to pick up the boat they have hired for the trip.

We had written for a boat—a double sculling skiff; and when we went down with our bags to the yard, and gave our names, the man said:

"Oh, yes; you're the party that wrote for a double sculling skiff. It's all right. Jim, fetch round *The Pride of the Thames*."

The boy went, and re-appeared five minutes afterwards, struggling with an **antediluvian** chunk of wood, that looked as though it had been recently dug out of somewhere, and dug out carelessly, so as to have been unnecessarily damaged in the process.

My own idea, on first catching sight of the object, was that it was a Roman relic of some sort,—relic of *what* I do not know, possibly of a coffin.

The neighbourhood of the upper Thames is rich in Roman relics, and my **surmise** seemed to me a very probable one; but our serious young man, who is a bit of a geologist, pooh-poohed my Roman relic theory, and said it was clear to the meanest intellect (in which category he seemed to be grieved that he could not conscientiously include mine) that the thing the boy had found was the fossil of a whale; and he pointed out to us various evidences proving that it must have belonged to the preglacial period.

To settle the dispute, we appealed to the boy. We told him not to be afraid, but to speak the plain truth: Was it the fossil of a **pre-Adamite** whale, or was it an early Roman coffin?

The boy said it was *The Pride of the Thames*.

We thought this a very humorous answer on the part of the boy at first, and somebody gave him twopence as a reward for his ready wit; but when he persisted in keeping up the joke, as we thought, too long, we got **vexed** with him.

"Come, come, my lad!" said our captain sharply, "don't let us have any nonsense. You take your mother's washing-tub home again, and bring us a boat."

The boat-builder himself came up then, and assured us, on his word, as a practical man, that the thing really was a boat—was, in fact, *the* boat, the "double sculling skiff" selected to take us on our trip down the river.

We grumbled a good deal. We thought he might, at least, have had it whitewashed or tarred—had *something* done to it to distinguish it from a bit of a wreck; but he could not see any fault in it.

He even seemed offended at our remarks. He said he had picked us out the best boat in all his stock, and he thought we might have been more grateful.

He said it, *The Pride of the Thames*, had been in use, just as it now stood (or rather as it now hung together), for the last forty years, to *his* knowledge, and nobody had complained of it before, and he did not see why we should be the first to begin.

We argued no more.

We fastened the so-called boat together with some pieces of string, got a bit of wall-paper and pasted over the shabbier places, said our prayers, and stepped on board.

They charged us thirty-five shillings for the loan of the remnant for six days; and we could have bought the thing out-and-out for four-and-sixpence at any sale of drift-wood round the coast.

---

antediluvian extremely old
surmise infer
pre-Adamite extremely old
vexed annoyed

Extract from *Travels in the Air* by James Glaisher

In the 19th century the only way to travel by air was by hot-air balloon. James Glaisher was a meteorologist and balloonist and the following extract describing a balloon trip over London is taken from his book *Travels in the Air*, which was first published in 1871.

Always, however great the height of the balloon, when I have seen the horizon it has roughly appeared to be on the level of the **car**—though of course the dip of the horizon is a very appreciable quantity—or the same height as the eye. From this one might infer that, could the earth be seen without a cloud or anything to obscure it, and the boundary line of the plane approximately the same height as the eye, the general appearance would be that of a slight concavity; but I have never seen any part of the surface of the earth other than as a plane. Towns and cities, when viewed from the balloon are like models in motion.

I shall always remember the ascent of 9th October, 1863, when we passed over London about sunset. At the time when we were 7,000 feet high, and directly over London Bridge, the scene around was one that cannot probably be equalled in the world. We were still so low as not to have lost sight of the details of the spectacle which presented itself to our eyes; and with one glance the homes of 3,000,000 people could be seen, and so distinct was the view, that every large building was easily distinguishable. In fact, the whole of London was visible, and some parts most clearly. All round, the suburbs were also very distinct, with their lines of detached villas, imbedded as it were in a mass of shrubs; beyond, the country was like a garden, its fields, well marked, becoming smaller and smaller as the eye wandered farther and farther away. Again looking down, there was the Thames, throughout its whole length, without the slightest mist, dotted over its winding course with innumerable ships and steamboats, like moving toys. Gravesend was visible, also the mouth of the Thames, and the coast around as far as Norfolk. The southern shore of the mouth of the Thames was not so clear, but the sea beyond was seen for many miles; when at a higher elevation, I looked for the coast of France, but was unable to see it. On looking round, the eye was arrested by the garden-like appearance of the county of Kent, till again London claimed yet more careful attention.

Smoke, thin and blue, was curling from it, and slowly moving away in beautiful curves, from all except one part, south of the Thames, where it was less blue and seemed more dense, till the cause became evident; it was mixed with mist rising from the ground, the southern limit of which was bounded by an even line, doubtless indicating the meeting of the subsoils of gravel and clay. The whole scene was surmounted by a canopy of blue, everywhere free from cloud, except near the horizon, where a band of cumulus and stratus extended all round, forming a fitting boundary to such a glorious view.

As seen from the earth, the sunset this evening was described as fine, the air being clear and the shadows well defined; but, as we rose to view it and its effects, the golden hues increased in intensity; their richness decreased as the distance from the sun increased, both right and left; but still as far as 90° from the sun, rose-coloured clouds extended. The remainder of the circle was completed, for the most part, by pure white cumulus of well-rounded and symmetrical forms.

I have seen London by night. I have crossed it during the day at the height of four miles. I have often admired the splendour of sky scenery, but never have I seen anything which surpassed this spectacle. The roar of the town heard at this elevation was a deep, rich, continuous sound—the voice of labour. At four miles above London, all was hushed; no sound reached our ears.

---

car the basket of a balloon

Crime and punishment

In Great Britain, the 19th century saw rising levels of crime. To combat public fears about the safety of London's streets, Sir Robert Peel established a professional, full-time police force – the Metropolitan Police – to enforce law and order. From street thieves to gang fights, many of the Victorians' concerns about crime echoed concerns that are expressed today.

Convicted criminals faced harsh punishments including hard labour, floggings and even hanging for the most serious crimes. In the first half of the 19th century, convicts could face transportation to British colonies such as Australia and Bermuda where they would be forced to carry out back-breaking work whilst being kept imprisoned in harsh conditions. Back in Great Britain, prisoners might be jailed in the notorious Newgate Gaol or one of the disease-ridden prison ships anchored on the Thames. Any children convicted of a crime fared little better and it was only at the very end of the 19th century that the practice of jailing children in adult prisons came to an end.

Extract from *Routledge's Popular Guide to London*

> This extract is taken from *Routledge's Popular Guide to London*, a travel guide published in 1873. Here the authors of the guide present advice on how to avoid becoming a victim of crime when visiting the city.

In walking through the streets, avoid lingering in crowded thoroughfares, and *keep on the right-hand side of the footway.*

Never enter into conversation with men who wish to show you the way, offer to sell "smuggled cigars" or invite you to take a glass of ale or play a game at skittles.

If in doubt about the direction of any street or building, inquire at a respectable shop or of the nearest policeman.

Do not relieve street-beggars, and avoid bye-ways and poor neighbourhoods after dark.

Carry no more money about you than is necessary for the day's expenses. Look after your watch and chain, and take care of your pockets at the entrance to theatres, exhibitions, churches, and in the omnibuses and the streets.

Extract from a letter in *The Times* newspaper

The following extract is taken from a letter published in *The Times* newspaper on 5th March 1850 and warns readers of a pickpocket working on the streets of London.

Sir, As *The Times* is always open for the insertion of any remarks likely to caution the unwary or to put the unsuspecting on their guard against the numerous thefts and robberies committed daily in the streets of London, I am induced to ask you to insert a case which happened on Saturday last, and which I trust may serve as a warning to those of your lady readers who still carry purses in their pockets.

A young lady of very **prepossessing** appearance, a relation of the narrator's, was walking between 12 and 1 o'clock with another young lady, a friend of hers, in Albany-street, where she resides, when she was accosted by a boy about 11 years of age, who asked her in the most beseeching tones "to buy a few oranges of a poor orphan who hadn't a bit of bread to eat." She told him to go away, but he kept alongside, imploring assistance, and making some cutting remarks about "the ingratitude of the world in general and of young ladies in particular." As his manner became very troublesome the lady threatened to give him in charge of a policeman, and looked down every area to find one; but there was not one even there, and the boy kept up his sweet discourse and slight pushes alternately, until the lady reached her own door-step. It then occurred to her that in the boy's ardour to sell his oranges he might have taken her purse; her friend thought so too. A trembling hand was inserted into the pocket; the purse was gone, and so was the lady's happiness. She flew after the thief, who, knowing young ladies were not made for running, coolly deposited his basket on a door-step a little way off and ran away whistling. This brave young lady ran also, shouting "Stop thief! stop thief!" (but then young ladies are not made for shouting, God forbid!) and she looked in the fond hope that a policeman might be found. But no such luck, the culprit got safely off with the purse and its contents; and no kind passer by tried to help the young lady, who was thus shamefully duped and robbed. Ladies, young and old, never carry your purses in your pockets; beware of **canting** beggars, and beggars of all sorts, that infest the streets; and, above all, keep a watchful eye about you and give the widest possible berth to THE ORANGE BOY.

---

prepossessing attractive
canting pleading

Extract from *The Hooligan Nights* by Clarence Rook

FICTION

> The following extract is taken from *The Hooligan Nights*, first published in 1899. Here, the author describes an encounter with Young Alf, a young criminal who describes to him how to steal.

"Look 'ere," he said, "if you see a fing you want, you just go and take it wivout any 'anging abart. If you 'ang abart you draw suspicion, and you get lagged for loiterin' wiv intent to commit a felony or some dam nonsense like that. Go for it, strite. P'r'aps it's a 'awse and cart you see as'll do you fine. Jump up and drive away as 'ard as you can, and ten to one nobody'll say anyfink. They'll think it's your own prop'ty. But 'ang around, and you mit jest as well walk into the next cop you see, and arst 'im to 'and you your stretch. See? You got to look after yourself; and it ain't your graft to look after anyone else, nor it ain't likely that anybody else'd look after you - only the cops. See?"

A cloud came over the moon, and threw the room and the yard outside into darkness. Young Alf became a dim shadow against the window.

"Time we was off," he said.

He shut down the window softly, and, by the shaded light of a match with which I supplied him, led me to the door and down the stairs. The dog was awake and alert, and barked noisily, though young Alf's step would not have broken an egg or caused a hare to turn in its sleep. He protested in a whisper against my inability to tread a stair without bringing the house about my ears. But the yard outside was empty, and no one but the dog seemed aware of our presence. Young Alf was bound, he said, for the neighbourhood of Westminster Bridge, but he walked with me down to Vauxhall Station through a network of dim and silent streets.

I inquired of his plans for the night, and he explained that there was a bit of a street-fight in prospect. The Drury Lane boys were coming across the bridge, and had engaged to meet the boys from Lambeth Walk at a coffee-stall on the other side. Then one of the Lambeth boys would make to one of the Drury Lane boys a remark which cannot be printed, but never fails to send the monkey of a Drury Lane boy a considerable way up the pole. Whereafter the Drury Lane boys would fall upon the Lambeth boys, and the Lambeth boys would give them what for.

As we came under the gas-lamps of Upper Kennington Lane, young Alf opened his coat. He was prepared for conflict. Round his throat he wore the blue neckerchief, spotted with white, with which my memory will always associate him; beneath that a light jersey.

Diving into his breast pocket, and glancing cautiously round, he drew out a handy-looking chopper which he poised for a moment, as though assuring himself of its balance.

"That's awright, eh?" he said, putting the chopper in my hand.

"Are you going to fight with that?" I asked, handing it back to him.

He passed his hand carefully across the blade.

"That oughter mean forty winks for one or two of 'em. Don't you fink so?" he said.

His eyes glittered in the light of the gas-lamp as he thrust the chopper back into his pocket and buttoned up his coat, having first carefully smoothed down the ends of his spotted neckerchief.

"Then you'll have a late night, I suppose?" I said as we passed along up the lane.

"'Bout two o'clock I shall be back at my kip," he replied.

We parted for the night at Vauxhall Cross, where a small crowd of people waited for their trains. We did not shake hands. The ceremony always seems unfamiliar and embarrassing to him. With a curt nod he turned and slid through the crowd, a lithe, well-knit figure. shoulders slightly hunched, turning his head neither to this side nor to that, hands close to his trouser pockets, sneaking his way like a fish through the scattered peril of rocks.

Extract from *The Seven Curses of London* by James Greenwood

> The following extract is taken from *The Seven Curses of London*, a collection of journalism by James Greenwood, first published in 1869. Here, he lists some of the slang used by criminals in London.

There is a language current amongst them that is to be met with in no dictionary with which I am acquainted. I doubt if even the "slang dictionary" contains more than a few of the following instances that may be accepted as genuine. It will be seen that the prime essential of "thieves' latin" is brevity. By its use, much may in one or two words be conveyed to a comrade while rapidly passing him in the street, or, should opportunity serve, during a visit to him while in prison.

To erase the original name or number from a stolen watch, and substitute one that is fictitious— *christening Jack.*

To take the works from one watch, and case them in another— *churching Jack.*

Poultry stealing— *beak hunting.*

One who steals from the shopkeeper while pretending to effect an honest purchase— a *bouncer.*

One who entices another to play at a game at which cheating rules, such as card or skittle sharping— a *buttoner.*

The treadmill, *shin scraper* (arising, it may be assumed, on account of the operator's liability, if he is not careful, to get his shins scraped by the ever-revolving wheel).

To commit burglary— crack a *case,* or *break a drum.*

The van that conveys prisoners to gaol— *Black Maria.*

A thief who robs cabs or carriages by climbing up behind, and cutting the straps that secure the luggage on the roof— a *dragsman.*

Breaking a square of glass— *starring the glaze.*

Training young thieves— *kidsman.*

To be transported or sent to penal servitude— *lagged.*

Three years' imprisonment— a *stretch.*

Six months— *half stretch.*

Three months' imprisonment— a *tail piece.*

To rob a till— *pinch a bob.*

A confederate in the practice of thimble rigging— a *nobbler.*

One who assists at a sham street row for the purpose of creating a mob, and promoting robbery from the person— a *jolly.*

A thief who secretes goods in a shop while a confederate distracts the attention of the shopkeeper is— a *palmer.*

A person marked for plunder— *a plant.*

Going out to steal linen in process of drying in gardens— *going snowing.*

Bad money— *sinker.*

Passer of counterfeit coins— *smasher.*

Stolen property generally— *swag.*

To go about half-naked to excite compassion— *on the shallow.*

Stealing lead from the roof of houses— *flying the blue pigeon.*

Coiners of bad money— *bit fakers.*

Midnight prowlers who rob drunken men— *bug hunters.*

Entering a dwelling house while the family have gone to church — *a dead lurk.*

Convicted of thieving— *in for a vamp.*

A city missionary or scripture reader— *gospel grinder.*

Shop-lifting— *hoisting.*

Hidden from the police— *in lavender.*

Forged bank notes— *queer screens.*

Whipping while in prison— *scroby* or *claws for breakfast.*

Long-fingered thieves expert in emptying ladies' pockets— *fine wirers.*

The condemned call— *the salt box.*

The prison chaplain— *Lady Green.*

A boy thief, lithe and thin and daring, such a one as housebreakers hire for the purpose of entering a small window at the rear of a dwelling house— *a little snakesman.*

Extract from *Mysteries of London* by G. W. M. Reynolds

FICTION

'Penny dreadfuls' or 'penny bloods' were lurid and sensational serial stories of crime and mystery, published in parts over a number of weeks, with each part priced at one penny. These stories were popular with working-class readers and blamed by many for luring unsuspecting children into a life of crime. The following extract is taken from *The Mysteries of London*, a popular 'penny dreadful' published in 1845. Here, the hero of the story, Richard Markham, makes a night-time journey to the East End of London to meet the man who is blackmailing him.

It was now midnight; and the streets were nearly deserted. The lamps, few and far between, only made darkness visible, instead of throwing a useful light upon the intricate maze of narrow thoroughfares.

Markham's object was to reach Shoreditch as soon as possible; for he knew that opposite the church there was a cab-stand where he might procure a vehicle to take him home. Emerging from Brick Lane, he crossed Church Street, and struck into that labyrinth of dirty and dangerous lanes in the vicinity of Bird-cage Walk, which we alluded to at the commencement of the preceding chapter.

He soon perceived that he had mistaken his way; and at length found himself floundering about in a long narrow street, unpaved, and here and there almost blocked up with heaps of **putrescent** filth. There was not a lamp in this perilous thoroughfare no moon on high **irradiated** his path;- black night enveloped every thing above and below in total darkness.

Once or twice he thought he heard footsteps behind him; and then he stopped, hoping to be overtaken by some one of whom he might inquire his way. But either his ears deceived him, or else the person whose steps he heard stopped when he did.

There was not a light in any of the houses on either side; and not a sound of revelry or sorrow escaped from the ill-closed **casements**.

Richard was bewildered; and - to speak truly - he began to be alarmed. He remembered to have read of the mysterious disappearance of persons in the east end of the metropolis, and also of certain tell deeds of crime which had been lately brought to light in the very district where he was now wandering;- and he could not help wishing that he was in some more secure and less gloomy region. He was groping his way along, feeling with his hands against the houses to guide him, - now knee-deep in some filthy puddle, now stumbling over some heap of slimy dirt, now floundering up to his ankles in the mud, - when a heavy and crushing blow fell upon his hat from behind.

He staggered and fell against the door of a house. Almost at the same instant that door was thrust open, and two powerful arms hurled the prostrate young man down three or four steps into a passage. The person who thus ferociously attacked him leapt after him, closing the door violently behind him.

All this occupied but a couple of seconds; and though Markham was not completely stunned by the blow, he was too much stupefied by the suddenness and violence of the assault to cry out. To this circumstance he was probably indebted for his life for the villain who had struck him no doubt conceived the blow to have been fatal; and therefore, instead of renewing the attack, he strode over Markham and entered a room into which the passage opened.

Richard's first idea was to rise and attempt an escape by the front door; but before he had time to consider it even for a moment, the murderous ruffian struck a light in the room, which, as well as a part of the passage, was immediately illuminated by a powerful glare.

Markham had been thrown upon the damp tiles with which the passage was paved, in such a manner that his head was close by the door of the room. The man who had assailed him lighted a piece of candle in a bright tin shade hanging against the wall; and the reflection produced by the metal caused the strong glare that fell so suddenly upon Richard's eyes.

Markham was about to start from his prostrate position when the interior of that room was thus abruptly revealed to him; but for a few moments the spectacle which met his sight paralyzed every limb, and rendered him breathless, speechless, and motionless with horror.

Stretched upon a shutter, which three chairs supported, was a corpse - naked, and of that blueish or livid colour which denotes the beginning of decomposition!

Near this loathsome object was a large tub full of water; and to that part of the ceiling immediately above it were affixed two large hooks, to each of which hung thick cords.

In one corner of the room were long flexible iron rods, spades, pickaxes, wooden levers, coils of thick rope, trowels, saws, hammers, huge chisels, skeleton keys, etc.

But how great was Richard's astonishment when, glancing from the objects just described towards the ruffian who had hurled him into that den of horrors, his eyes were struck by the sombre and revolting countenance of the Resurrection Man.

---

putrescent decomposing
irradiated lit up
casements windows

Extract from an article in the magazine *Household Words*

> The following extract is taken from a magazine article written by an anonymous prisoner describing his first day in Newgate Gaol. This article was first published in the magazine *Household Words* in 1853.

Strong and stony as the prison seems to passers by, it looks much stonier and stronger to the men who enter it. The multiplicity of heavy walls, of iron gates and doorways; of huge locks, of bolts, spikes and bars of every imaginable shape and size, make of the place a very nightmare dungeon. I followed the gruff under-warden, through some dark and chilly vaulted passages, now turning to the right, now to the left. We crossed a large hall, in the centre of which is a glass room for the use of prisoners when they are giving instructions to their lawyers.

Still following, I was led into another large recess or chamber, on one side of which was a huge boiler with a furnace glowing under it, and on another side a large stone bath. On the third wall there were a couple of round towels on a roller, with a wooden bench beneath them.

"Stop," cried the warden, "take your clothes off." I hesitated. "Take off your clothes, do you hear?" My clothes were soon laid on the bench, and a hot bath filled, and I went in. The officer had then his opportunity of taking up my garments one by one, searching their pockets and their linings, feeling them about and holding them against the light. My boots appeared to be especially suspicious. After he had put his hands into them, he thumped them violently on the stone floor; but there rolled nothing out.

Having bathed, I was led down another passage, at the end of which were two gratings of iron bars, closely woven over with wire-work, distant about two feet from each other. Unlocking both he pushed me through, and started me up two or three steps into a square court-yard, where there was a man walking to and fro very violently. After shouting "One in!" he locked the two gratings, and retreated rapidly in the direction of his dinner. Another warden with a bunch of keys came from a gloomy building that formed one side of the court. "Go up," he said to the pedestrian; who disappeared up a staircase instantly.

"Where are you from?" the jailor asked me, and "What are you here for?" Being replied to on these points, he said shortly, "Come this way." He led up the dark stone staircase to a corridor with cells on one side, having iron doors to them a foot or more in thickness. One of those cells was to be mine. Venturing as I went in to ask "Whether I might be allowed to walk in the yard when I pleased?" he answered sharply," You'll just please to walk where and when you're told." He slammed the door, bolted it, locked, and padlocked it.

The cell was about eight feet by four, lighted by a loophole above eye-level. It contained, besides an iron bedstead with a straw mattress and two coarse rugs upon it, an uncomfortable stool and a slanting reading-desk fastened to the wall, on which were a Bible, a prayer-book, and hymn-book. Alone for the first time since my apprehension, I stretched myself upon the bed; and, with my hands over my eyes endeavoured to collect my thoughts.

I was soon aroused by the undoing of bolts and bars below, while a **stentorian** voice shouted from the yard, "All — down!" I heard the cell doors being opened in the corridor; and, in due turn mine was flung open, and the jailor looked in. The impression my body had left upon the rugs enraged him dreadfully. "What," he cried, almost in a scream, "you've been a lying on that 'ere bed, have you! You just let me catch you on it again till night, that's all!"

"Oh," I said soothingly, "I didn't know. Now that I do know, I will not lie down again."

"If I find you on it again I'll have you up before the governor or stop your supper. That's all. Go down."

---

stentorian extremely loud

Extract from a letter in *The Daily Chronicle* newspaper

In the Victorian era, children who were convicted of a crime could find themselves sent to adult prisons. The following extract is taken from a letter the author Oscar Wilde wrote to *The Daily Chronicle* newspaper in 1897 after his own release from Reading prison and shows his concern about the treatment of children in prison.

Sir, I learn with great regret, through the columns of your paper, that the warder Martin, of Reading Prison, has been dismissed by the Prison Commissioners for having given some sweet biscuits to a little hungry child. I saw the three children myself on Monday preceding my release. They had just been convicted and were standing in a row in the central hall in their prison dress, carrying their sheets under the arms, previous to their being sent to the cells allotted to them.

They were quite small children, the youngest — the one to whom the warder gave the biscuits — being a tiny little chap, for whom they had evidently been unable to find clothes small enough to fit. I had, of course, seen many children in prison during the two years during which I was myself confined. Wandsworth Prison, especially, contained always a large number of children. But the little child I saw on the afternoon of Monday the 17th at Reading, was tinier than any one of them.

I need not say how utterly distressed I was to see these children at Reading, for I knew the treatment in store for them. The cruelty that is practised by day and night on children in English prisons is incredible, except to those who have witnessed it and are aware of the brutality of the system.

The terror of a child in prison is quite limitless. I remember once, in Reading, as I was going out to exercise, seeing in the dimly-lit cell right opposite my own, a small boy. Two warders — not unkindly men — were talking to him with some sternness apparently, or perhaps giving him some useful advice about his conduct. One was in the cell with him, the other was standing outside. The child's face was like a white wedge of sheer terror. There was in his eyes the terror of a hunted animal.

The next morning I heard him at breakfast time crying and calling to be let out. His cry was for his parents. From time to time I could hear the deep voice of the warder on duty telling him to keep quiet. Yet he was not even convicted of whatever little offence he had been charged with. He was simply on remand. That I knew by his wearing his own clothes, which seemed neat enough. He was, however, wearing prison socks and shoes. This showed that he was a very poor boy, whose own shoes, if he had any, were in a bad state. Justices and magistrates, an entirely ignorant class as a rule, often remand children for a week, and then perhaps remit whatever sentence they are entitled to pass. They call this "not sending a child to prison". It is, of course, a stupid view on their part. To a little child whether he is in prison on remand, or after conviction is not a subtlety of social position he can comprehend. To him the horrible thing is to be there at all. In the eyes of humanity it should be a horrible thing for him to be there at all.

Town and country

In the 19th century the populations of towns and cities grew rapidly as people moved from the countryside to urban areas in search of work. In 1801 the population of London was one million, but by the end of the century 6.7 million people called the city their home. From morning until night the busy streets were thronged with workers, beggars and the wealthy; people from every walk of life mixing on the streets of the teeming metropolis.

In Victorian times, the unspoilt beauty of the countryside couldn't disguise the hard lives of the people who lived and worked there. The Industrial Revolution also transformed the rural landscape with the coming of the railways and the introduction of machinery and steam changing countryside practices that previously had endured for centuries.

Extract from *The Adventure of the Copper Beeches* by Arthur Conan Doyle

The following extract is taken from the short story, *The Adventure of the Copper Beeches*, which was first published in 1892. Here, Sherlock Holmes and Dr Watson are travelling to the Hampshire countryside to meet their client, Miss Hunter, and Sherlock Holmes sets out his views about the dangers of the countryside.

By eleven o'clock the next day we were well upon our way to the old English capital. Holmes had been buried in the morning papers all the way down, but after we had passed the Hampshire border he threw them down and began to admire the scenery. It was an ideal spring day, a light blue sky, flecked with little fleecy white clouds drifting across from west to east. The sun was shining very brightly, and yet there was an exhilarating nip in the air, which set an edge to a man's energy. All over the countryside, away to the rolling hills around Aldershot, the little red and gray roofs of the farmsteadings peeped out from amid the light green of the new foliage.

"Are they not fresh and beautiful?" I cried with all the enthusiasm of a man fresh from the fogs of Baker Street.

But Holmes shook his head gravely.

"Do you know, Watson," said he, "that it is one of the curses of a mind with a turn like mine that I must look at everything with reference to my own special subject. You look at these scattered houses, and you are impressed by their beauty. I look at them, and the only thought which comes to me is a feeling of their isolation and of the impunity with which crime may be committed there."

"Good heavens!" I cried. "Who would associate crime with these dear old homesteads?"

"They always fill me with a certain horror. It is my belief, Watson, founded upon my experience, that the lowest and vilest alleys in London do not present a more dreadful record of sin than does the smiling and beautiful countryside."

"You horrify me!"

"But the reason is very obvious. The pressure of public opinion can do in the town what the law cannot accomplish. There is no lane so vile that the scream of a tortured child, or the thud of a drunkard's blow, does not **beget** sympathy and indignation among the neighbours, and then the whole machinery of justice is ever so close that a word of complaint can set it going, and there is but a step between the crime and the dock. But look at these lonely houses, each in its own fields, filled for the most part with poor ignorant folk who know little of the law. Think of the deeds of hellish cruelty, the hidden wickedness which may go on, year in, year out, in such places, and none the wiser. Had this lady who appeals to us for help gone to live in Winchester, I should never have had a fear for her. It is the five miles of country which makes the danger."

beget produce

Article from *Blackwoods Magazine*

The following article describing 24 hours in the city of London was published in *Blackwoods Magazine* in August 1841.

Towards midnight two or three thousands of your fellow creatures have been snatching hours from rest, to cart and pack the vegetables that will form a portion of your principal meal; and, if you are wakeful, the ponderous rumbling of waggon wheels over the rocky pavement, **apprize** you of this transit to the vast emporium of Covent Garden. From the north, droves of sheep, oxen and swine, directed by the steady herdsman and the sagacious dog, thread their way to Smithfield, where, long before dawn, they are safely penned, awaiting the purchase of the salesmen of Leadenhall and Newgate markets.

The river, in the dead hour of night, is alive with boats, conveying every variety of the finny tribe to Billingsgate; now are the early breakfast houses reaping their harvest, the bustling host, in his shirt sleeves, conveying refreshment to his numerous customers; now the footstep of the policeman, as he tramps slowly over his beat, awakes the slumbering echoes; every house is shrouded in **repose**, and the city seems a city of the dead. All, soon again, is noise, bustle and confusion; the carts of thousands of fishmongers, green-grocers, and victuallers, rattle along the streets, taking up their stands in orderly array in the immediate vicinity of the respective markets. In a little while, however, they have completed their cargo for the day, and drive off; the waggons disappear, the markets are swept clean, and no trace remains.

Five o'clock gives some little signs of life in the vicinity of the hotels and coach-offices; a two-horse stage, or railway "bus" rumbles off to catch the early trains; the street-retailers of fish, vegetables and fruit may be encountered, bearing on their heads their respective stocks in trade.

Six o'clock announces the beginning of the working day, by the ringing of the bells of various manufactories. Now is the street crowded with the **fustian-coated** artizan, his basket of tools in his hand; and the stalwart Irish labourer, his short black pipe scenting the morning air with odours; the newspaper offices, busy during the night, now "let off" their gas - the sub-editors and compositors go home to bed, leaving the pressmen to complete the labour of the night.

There is an **interregnum** until eight; the shopkeeper

then begins his day, the porter taking down the shutters, the boy sweeping out the shop and the **slipshod** prentice lounging about the door; the principal comes in from his country box about nine; the assistants have then breakfasted and dressed; and at ten the real business of the day begins.

At ten, too, the stream of life begins to set in city-ways; the rich merchant from Hampstead and Camberwell dashes along in his well-appointed curricle; the cashier, managing director, and principal accountant, reaches his place of business comfortably seated in his **gig**; clerks of all denominations foot it from Hackney, Islington and Peckham Rye; the "busses" are filled with a motley crew of all descriptions, from Paddington, Piccadilly, Elephant and Castle, and Mile-End.

From eleven till two the tide of population sets in strongly city-ways; then, when the greater part of the business in that quarter has been transaction, the West End tradesmen begin to open their eyes and look about them; although in Regent Street business is not at its maximum until four or five o'clock, and soon after the city is almost deserted. About two, all over London there is a lull; important business, that brooks no delay, must then be transacted - the vital business of dinner; for an hour little or nothing is done and no sound man of business expects to do any thing. Dinner over, business recommences with the energy of giants refreshed. About six o'clock the great business of the city is totally at an end; the tide is then a tide of ebb setting out through all the avenues of town to the westward and to the suburbs. Now eating begins in West End, and drinking in city taverns; now the coffeehouses fill and crowds gather round the doors of the theatres, patiently awaiting for an hour or more the opening of the doors.

Nine o'clock and the shops begin to close, save those of the cigar dealers and gin-spinners, whose business is now only about to begin; the streets swarm with young men about town, and loose characters of all descriptions issue from their hiding-places.

About midnight the continuous roll of carriages indicates the breaking up of the theatrical **auditories**, while the streets are crowded with respectable persons hastening to their houses; one o'clock and all is shut up, save the watering-houses opposite the hackney coach and cab stands, the subterranean singing rooms, the a la mode beef houses, lobster taverns and ham shops at two the day may be said to end.

---

apprize tell
repose rest
saloop a hot drink popular in the 19th century
fustian-coated a heavy cloth coat
interregnum pause
slipshod careless
gig a type of horse-drawn carriage
auditories auditoriums

Extract from *The Woman in White* by Wikie Collins

FICTION

In the following extract from the novel *The Woman in White*, first published in 1859, a young man called Walter Hartright is walking home from Hampstead in London when he meets a mysterious woman.

I had now arrived at that particular point of my walk where four roads met—the road to Hampstead, along which I had returned, the road to Finchley, the road to West End, and the road back to London. I had mechanically turned in this latter direction, and was strolling along the lonely high-road—idly wondering, I remember, what the Cumberland young ladies would look like—when, in one moment, every drop of blood in my body was brought to a stop by the touch of a hand laid lightly and suddenly on my shoulder from behind me.

I turned on the instant, with my fingers tightening round the handle of my stick.

There, in the middle of the broad bright high-road— there, as if it had that moment sprung out of the earth or dropped from the heaven—stood the figure of a solitary Woman, dressed from head to foot in white garments, her face bent in grave inquiry on mine, her hand pointing to the dark cloud over London, as I faced her.

I was far too seriously startled by the suddenness with which this extraordinary apparition stood before me, in the dead of night and in that lonely place, to ask what she wanted. The strange woman spoke first.

"Is that the road to London?" she said.

I looked attentively at her, as she put that **singular** question to me. It was then nearly one o'clock. All I could discern distinctly by the moonlight was a colourless, youthful face, meagre and sharp to look at about the cheeks and chin; large, grave, wistfully attentive eyes; nervous, uncertain lips; and light hair of a pale, brownish-yellow hue. There was nothing wild, nothing immodest in her manner: it was quiet and self-controlled, a little melancholy and a little touched by suspicion; not exactly the manner of a lady, and, at the same time, not the manner of a woman in the humblest rank of life. The voice, little as I had yet heard of it, had something curiously still and mechanical in its tones, and the utterance was remarkably rapid. She held a small bag in her hand: and her dress—bonnet, shawl, and gown all of white—was, so far as I could guess, certainly not composed of very delicate or very expensive materials. Her figure was slight, and rather above the average height—her gait and actions free from the slightest approach to extravagance. This was all that I could observe of her in the dim light and under the perplexingly strange circumstances of our meeting. What sort of a woman she was, and how she came to be out alone in the high-road, an hour after midnight, I altogether failed to guess. The one thing of which I felt certain was, that the grossest of mankind could not have misconstrued her motive in speaking, even at that suspiciously late hour and in that suspiciously lonely place.

"Did you hear me?" she said, still quietly and rapidly, and without the least fretfulness or impatience. "I asked if that was the way to London."

singular remarkable

Extract from *Picturesque Sketches of London Past and Present* by Thomas Miller

In 19th-century London, thick fogs were often caused by the high levels of air pollution. This type of weather became known as 'pea soup fog' due to its thickness and consistency and this extract from *Picturesque Sketches of London Past and Present*, first published in 1852, describes a typical London fog.

Such of our readers as have never been in London in November can scarcely imagine what it is to grope their way through a downright thorough London fog. It is something like being imbedded in a dilution of yellow peas-pudding, just thick enough to get through it without being wholly choked or completely suffocated. You can see through the yard of it which, at the next stride, you are doomed to swallow, and that is all. It is a kind of meat and drink, and very sorry sustenance for those who are asthmatical, as you may tell by hearing one old cough answering to another from opposite sides of the street, and which, although you cannot see the passengers, you can tell, from their grumbling, that they do not like the fare at all. You have the same soft-soapy atmosphere served up at breakfast, dinner, tea, and supper; every time you open your mouth you partake of it, and all day long you are compelled to burn lights, and, in addition to the fog, inhale the fumes from gas, candle, or lamp, which have no more chance of escape than you have, so burn on dim, yellow, and sulkily, as if the very lights needed all the warmth they could obtain, and thus confine themselves to illuminating the smallest possible space. The whole city seems covered with a crust, and all the light you can see beneath it appears as if struggling through the huge yellow basin it overspreads. You fancy that all the smoke which had ascended for years from the thousands of London chimneys had fallen down all at once, after having rotted somewhere above the clouds; smelling as if it had been kept too long, and making you wheeze and sneeze as if all the colds in the world were rushing into your head for warmth, and did not care a straw about killing a few thousands of people, so long as they could but lodge comfortably for a few hours anywhere. You seem as if you had swallowed six broken-winded horses; that they were inside of you alive and kicking; and, for the soul of you, you cannot get rid of one.

You step gingerly along, feeling your way beside the walls, windows, and doors, whenever you can, until at last you tumble headlong into some cellar -

perhaps on the shoulders of the little cobbler who is at work below, and who chances to have his sharp **awl** uplifted at the moment; or perhaps it is an underground coal-shed, and you alight on the back of the black-looking woman weighing coals, and double her up in her own scale - receiving, in return, a couple of black eyes from her husband. After a hearty **drubbing**, you escape once more into the street; and, as you cannot see a yard before you, break your shins over a milkman's can, and upset the contents on the greasy pavement; he tries to collar you, but your blood is now up, and you give him a "straight-armer," which sends him into the area, upsetting the fat cook as he falls. You then run for it, and come full butt against the "bow-window" of a respectable old gentleman, with whom you have a roll or two in the gutter, thankful that you did not fall on the other side, and stave in the shop-front. You shake yourself, and are glad that you are as you are; for a foot beyond where you fell there yawns an open grating, beneath which runs the huge sewer that empties itself into the Thames; and you wonder how many have slipt in during the day.

---

awl a pointed tool
drubbing beating

Letter in *The Morning Chronicle* newspaper

In the following letter, published in *The Morning Chronicle* on 11th April 1850, Henry Mayhew describes his view of a fog-bound London from the Golden Gallery at the top of St. Paul's Cathedral.

In the hope of obtaining a bird's-eye view of the port, I went up to the Golden Gallery that is immediately below the ball of St. Paul's. It was noon, and an exquisitely bright and clear spring day; but the view was smudgy and smeared with smoke. And yet the haze which hung like a curtain of shadow before and over everything, increased rather than diminished the giant **sublimity** of the city that lay stretched out beneath.

It was utterly unlike London as seen every day below, in all its bricken and hard-featured reality; it was rather the **phantasm** - the spectral illusion, as it were, of the great metropolis - such as one might see it in a dream, with here and there stately churches and **palatial** hospitals, shimmering like white marble, their windows glittering in the sunshine like plates of burnished gold - while the rest of the scene was all hazy and indefinite.

Even the outlines of the neighbouring streets, steeples, and towers were blurred in misty indistinctness. Clumps of buildings and snatches of parks loomed through the clouds like dim islands rising out of the sea of smoke. It was impossible to tell where the sky ended and the city began; and as you peered into the thick haze you could, after a time, make out the dusky figures of tall factory chimneys plumed with black smoke; while spires and turrets seemed to hang midway between you and the earth, as if poised in the thick grey air. In the distance the faint hills, with the sun shining upon them, appeared like some far-off shore, or a mirage seen in the sky - indeed, the whole scene was more like the view of some imaginary and romantic Cloudland, than that of the most matter-of-fact and prosaic city in the world. As you peeped down into the thoroughfares you could see streams of busy little men, like ants, continually hurrying along in opposite directions; while, what with carts, cabs, and omnibuses, the earth seemed all alive with tiny creeping things, as when one looks into the grass on a summer's day. As you listened you caught the roar of the restless human tide of enterprise and competition at work below; and as you turned to contemplate the river at your back, you saw the sunlight shining upon the grey water beneath you like a sheet of golden tissue, while far away in the distance it sparkled again as the stream went twisting through the monster town. Beyond London-bridge

162

nothing was visible; a thick veil of haze and fog hung before the shipping, so that not one solitary mast was to be seen marking the far-famed port of London. And yet one would hardly have had it otherwise! To behold the metropolis without its smoke - with its thousand steeples standing out against the clear blue sky, sharp and definite in their outlines - is to see London as it is *not* - without its native element. But as the vast city lay there beneath me, half hid in mist and with only glimpses of its greatness visible, it had a much more sublime and ideal effect from the very inability to grasp the whole of its literal reality.

sublimity majestic
phantasm an illusion
palatial looking like a palace

Extract from *The Return of the Native* by Thomas Hardy

The following extract is taken from the novel *The Return of the Native*, which was first published in 1878. Here, as twilight approaches, the author describes Egdon Heath, a rural area in the fictional county of Wessex mainly inhabited by workers who cut the furze (gorse) that grows there.

A Saturday afternoon in November was approaching the time of twilight, and the vast tract of unenclosed wild known as Egdon Heath **embrowned** itself moment by moment. Overhead the hollow stretch of whitish cloud shutting out the sky was as a tent which had the whole heath for its floor.

The heaven being spread with this **pallid** screen and the earth with the darkest vegetation, their meeting-line at the horizon was clearly marked. In such contrast the heath wore the appearance of an instalment of night which had taken up its place before its astronomical hour was come: darkness had to a great extent arrived **hereon**, while day stood distinct in the sky. Looking upwards, a furze-cutter would have been inclined to continue work; looking down, he would have decided to finish [...] and go home. The distant rims of the world and of the **firmament** seemed to be a division in time no less than a division in matter. The face of the heath by its mere complexion added half an hour to evening; it could in like manner **retard** the dawn, sadden noon, anticipate the frowning of storms scarcely generated, and intensify the opacity of a moonless midnight to a cause of shaking and dread.

In fact, precisely at this transitional point of its nightly roll into darkness the great and particular glory of the Egdon waste began, and nobody could be said to understand the heath who had not been there at such a time. It could best be felt when it could not clearly be seen, its complete effect and explanation lying in this and the succeeding hours before the next dawn; then, and only then, did it tell its true tale. The spot was, indeed, a near relation of night, and when night showed itself an apparent tendency to gravitate together could be perceived in its shades and the scene. The sombre stretch of rounds and hollows seemed to rise and meet the evening gloom in pure sympathy, the heath exhaling darkness as rapidly as the heavens precipitated it. And so the obscurity in the air and the obscurity in the land closed together in a black fraternization towards which each advanced halfway.

The place became full of a watchful intentness now; for when other things sank blooding to sleep the heath appeared slowly to awake and listen.

---

embrowned turned brown
pallid pale, lacking colour
hereon on this
firmament sky
retard slow down

Science and wonder

The 19th century was a time of great advances in science. From the invention of the steam engine to the discovery of the atom, scientific achievements transformed people's lives and the way they looked at the world.

At the beginning of the 19th century, scientists began to harness the power of electricity, with their strange experiments inspiring novels such as Mary Shelley's *Frankenstein.* The invention of the telegraph and later the telephone revolutionized long-distance communication, whilst the birth of photography and film at this time enables us to look back now at images of 19th-century life.

The publication of Charles Darwin's groundbreaking theory of evolution in 1859 revolutionized scientists' understanding of life on earth, whilst the discovery of X-rays, asteroids and radioactivity transformed their understanding of the universe. At the end of the 19th century, as science made even greater leaps forward into the unknown, authors such as H. G. Wells capitalized on the public's thirst for stories of science and wonder.

Extract from *A Study in Scarlet* by Arthur Conan Doyle

FICTION

> The following extract is taken from the novel *A Study in Scarlet*, which was first published in 1887. Here, Dr Watson is introduced to Sherlock Holmes for the first time by their mutual friend Stamford, and the detective describes the results of his latest scientific experiments.

As he spoke, we turned down a narrow lane and passed through a small side-door, which opened into a wing of the great hospital. It was familiar ground to me, and I needed no guiding as we ascended the bleak stone staircase and made our way down the long corridor with its vista of whitewashed wall and dun-coloured doors. Near the further end a low arched passage branched away from it and led to the chemical laboratory.

This was a lofty chamber, lined and littered with countless bottles. Broad, low tables were scattered about, which bristled with retorts, test-tubes, and little Bunsen lamps, with their blue flickering flames. There was only one student in the room, who was bending over a distant table absorbed in his work. At the sound of our steps he glanced round and sprang to his feet with a cry of pleasure. "I've found it! I've found it," he shouted to my companion, running towards us with a test-tube in his hand. "I have found a re-agent which is **precipitated** by **haemoglobin**, and by nothing else." Had he discovered a gold mine, greater delight could not have shone upon his features.

"Dr. Watson, Mr. Sherlock Holmes," said Stamford, introducing us.

"How are you?" he said cordially, gripping my hand with a strength for which I should hardly have given him credit. "You have been in Afghanistan, I perceive."

"How on earth did you know that?" I asked in astonishment.

"Never mind," said he, chuckling to himself. "The question now is about haemoglobin. No doubt you see the significance of this discovery of mine?"

"It is interesting, chemically, no doubt," I answered, "but practically — "

"Why, man, it is the most practical medico-legal discovery for years. Don't you see that it gives us an infallible test for blood stains. Come over here now!" He seized me by the coat-sleeve in his eagerness, and drew me over to the table at which he had been working. "Let us have some fresh blood," he said, digging a long bodkin into his finger, and drawing off the resulting drop of blood in a chemical pipette. "Now, I add this small quantity of blood to a litre of water. You perceive that the resulting mixture has the appearance of pure water. The proportion of blood cannot be more than one in a million. I have no doubt, however, that we shall be able to obtain the characteristic reaction." As he spoke, he threw into the vessel a few white crystals, and then added some drops of a transparent fluid. In an instant the contents assumed a dull mahogany colour, and a brownish dust was precipitated to the bottom of the glass jar.

"Ha! ha!" he cried, clapping his hands, and looking as delighted as a child with a new toy. "What do you think of that?"

"It seems to be a very delicate test," I remarked.

"Beautiful! beautiful! The old Guiacum test was very clumsy and uncertain. So is the microscopic examination for blood corpuscles. The latter is valueless if the stains are a few hours old. Now, this appears to act as well whether the blood is old or new. Had this test been invented, there are hundreds of men now walking the earth who would long ago have paid the penalty of their crimes."

"Indeed!" I murmured.

"Criminal cases are continually hinging upon that one point. A man is suspected of a crime months perhaps after it has been committed. His linen or clothes are examined, and brownish stains discovered upon them. Are they blood stains, or mud stains, or rust stains, or fruit stains, or what are they? That is a question which has puzzled many an expert, and why? Because there was no reliable test. Now we have the Sherlock Holmes' test, and there will no longer be any difficulty."

His eyes fairly glittered as he spoke, and he put his hand over his heart and bowed as if to some applauding crowd conjured up by his imagination.

"You are to be congratulated," I remarked, considerably surprised at his enthusiasm.

"There was the case of Von Bischoff at Frankfort last year. He would certainly have been hung had this test been in existence. Then there was Mason of Bradford, and the notorious Muller, and Lefevre of Montpellier, and Samson of New Orleans. I could name a score of cases in which it would have been decisive."

"You seem to be a walking calendar of crime," said Stamford with a laugh. "You might start a paper on those lines. Call it the `Police News of the Past.'"

"Very interesting reading it might be made, too," remarked Sherlock Holmes, sticking a small piece of plaster over the prick on his finger. "I have to be careful," he continued, turning to me with a smile, "for I dabble with poisons a good deal." He held out his hand as he spoke, and I noticed that it was all mottled over with similar pieces of plaster, and discoloured with strong acids.

---

precipitated separated in a solution
haemoglobin a protein that gives red blood cells their colour

Eyewitness accounts of public scientific experiments

In the 19th century, the invention of electrical batteries allowed scientists to experiment with the power of electricity. The Italian scientist Giovanni Aldini performed a series of experiments in public where he applied electrical currents to the corpses of convicted criminals. The following extract is taken from reports of his experiments in 1803.

A very ample series of experiments were made by Professor Aldini which show the eminent and superior power of **galvanism** beyond any other stimulant in nature. In the months of January and February last, he had the courage to apply it at Bologna to the bodies of various criminals who had suffered death at that place, and by means of the pile he excited the remaining vital forces in a most astonishing manner. This stimulus produced the most horrible contortions and grimaces by the motions of the muscles of the head and face; and an hour and a quarter after death, the arm of one of the bodies was elevated eight inches from the table on which it was supported, and this even when a considerable weight was placed in the hand.

George Forster was hung at 8am on 18th January 1803 at Newgate Prison, for the drowning of his wife and youngest child in the Paddington Canal. After hanging for an hour in sub-zero temperatures, Aldini **procured** the body and began his galvanic experiments.

On the first application of the process to the face, the jaws of the deceased criminal began to quiver, and the adjoining muscles were horribly contorted, and one eye was actually opened. In the subsequent part of the process the right hand was raised and clenched, and the legs and thighs were set in motion. Mr Pass, the beadle of the Surgeons' Company, who was officially present during this experiment, was so alarmed that he died of fright soon after his return home.

The action even of those muscles furthest distant from the points of contact with the arc was so much increased as almost to give an appearance of re-animation vitality might, perhaps, have been restored, if many circumstances had not rendered it impossible."

"Galvanism was communicated by means of three troughs combined together, each of which contained forty plates of zinc, and as many of copper. On the first application of the arcs the jaw began to quiver, the adjoining muscles were horribly contorted, and the left eye actually opened."

"The first of these decapitated criminals being conveyed to the apartment provided for my experiments, in the neighbourhood of the place of execution, the head was first subjected to the Galvanic action. For this purpose I had constructed a pile consisting of a hundred pieces of silver and zinc. Having moistened the inside of the ears with salt water, I formed an arc with two metallic wires, which, proceeding from the two ears, were applied, one to the summit and the other to the bottom of the pile. When this communication was established, I observed strong contractions in the muscles of the face, which were contorted in so irregular a manner that they exhibited the appearance of the most horrid grimaces. The action of the eye-lids was exceedingly striking, though less sensible in the human head than in that of an ox."

galvanism electrical stimulation
procured obtained

Extract from the introduction to *Frankenstein* by Mary Shelley

> The following extract is taken from the introduction Mary Shelley wrote to her novel *Frankenstein*, which was first published in 1818. Whilst on holiday in Switzerland with her husband and friends, the group decided to have a competition to see who could write the best horror story. Here, she describes how their discussion of the scientific experiments using electricity that were being carried out at that time helped to inspire her novel *Frankenstein*.

Perhaps a corpse would be re-animated; **galvanism** had given token of such things: perhaps the component parts of a creature might be manufactured, brought together, and **endued** with vital warmth.

Night waned upon this talk, and even the witching hour had gone by, before we retired to rest. When I placed my head on my pillow, I did not sleep, nor could I be said to think. My imagination, unbidden, possessed and guided me, gifting the successive images that arose in my mind with a vividness far beyond the usual bounds of **reverie**. I saw with shut eyes, but acute mental vision, I saw the pale student of **unhallowed** arts kneeling beside the thing he had put together. I saw the hideous **phantasm** of a man stretched out, and then, on the working of some powerful engine, show signs of life, and stir with an uneasy, half vital motion. Frightful must it be; for supremely frightful would be the effect of any human endeavour to mock the stupendous mechanism of the Creator of the world. His success would terrify the artist; he would rush away from his odious handywork, horror-stricken. He would hope that, left to itself, the slight spark of life which he had communicated would fade; that this thing, which had received such imperfect animation, would subside into dead matter; and he might sleep in the belief that the silence of the grave would quench for ever the transient existence of the hideous corpse which he had looked upon as the cradle of life. He sleeps; but he is awakened; he opens his eyes; behold the horrid thing stands at his bedside, opening his curtains, and looking on him with yellow, watery, but speculative eyes.

I opened mine in terror. The idea so possessed my mind, that a thrill of fear ran through me, and I wished to exchange the ghastly image of my fancy for the realities around. I see them still; the very room, the dark *parquet*, the closed shutters, with the moonlight struggling through, and the sense I had that the glassy lake and white high Alps were beyond. I could not so easily get rid of my hideous phantom; still it haunted me. I must try to think of something else. I recurred to my ghost story, my tiresome unlucky ghost story! O! if I could only contrive one which would frighten my reader as I myself had been frightened that night!

Swift as light and as cheering was the idea that broke in upon me. "I have found it! What terrified me will terrify others; and I need only describe the spectre which had haunted my midnight pillow." On the morrow I announced that I had thought of a story. I began that day with the words, *It was on a dreary night of November,* making only a transcript of the grim terrors of my waking dream.

---

galvanism electrical stimulation
endued provided
reverie a state of dreaming
unhallowed unholy
phantasm phantom, apparition

Extract from *Frankenstein* by Mary Shelley

In this extract from the novel *Frankenstein*, first published in 1818, Victor Frankenstein brings the creature he has created to life.

It was on a dreary night of November that I beheld the accomplishment of my toils. With an anxiety that almost amounted to agony, collected the instruments of life around me, that I might infuse a spark of being into the lifeless thing that lay at my feet. It was already one in the morning; the rain pattered dismally against the panes, and my candle was nearly burnt out, when, by the glimmer of the half-extinguished light, I saw the dull yellow eye of the creature open; it breathed hard, and a convulsive motion **agitated** its limbs.

How can I describe my emotions at this catastrophe, or how **delineate** the wretch whom with such infinite pains and care I had endeavoured to form? His limbs were in proportion, and I had selected his features as beautiful. Beautiful! Great God! His yellow skin scarcely covered the work of muscles and arteries beneath; his hair was of a lustrous black, and flowing; his teeth of a pearly whiteness;

but these **luxuriances** only formed a more horrid contrast with his watery eyes, that seemed almost of the same colour as the dun-white sockets in which they were set, his shrivelled complexion and straight black lips.

The different accidents of life are not so changeable as the feelings of human nature. I had worked hard for nearly two years, for the sole purpose of infusing life into an inanimate body. For this I had deprived myself of rest and health. I had desired it with an **ardour** that far exceeded moderation; but now that I had finished, the beauty of the dream vanished, and breathless horror and disgust filled my heart. Unable to endure the aspect of the being I had created, I rushed out of the room and continued a long time **traversing** my bed-chamber, unable to compose my mind to sleep. At length **lassitude** succeeded to the tumult I had before endured, and I threw myself on the bed in my clothes, endeavouring to seek a few moments of forgetfulness. But it was in vain; I slept, indeed, but I was disturbed by the wildest dreams. I thought I saw Elizabeth, in the bloom of health, walking in the streets of **Ingolstadt**. Delighted and surprised, I embraced her, but as I imprinted the first kiss on her lips, they became livid with the hue of death; her features appeared to change, and I thought that I held the corpse of my dead mother in my arms; a shroud enveloped her form, and I saw the grave-worms crawling in the folds of the flannel. I started from my sleep with horror; a cold dew covered my forehead, my teeth chattered, and every limb became convulsed; when, by the dim and yellow light of the moon, as it forced its way through the window shutters, I beheld the wretch—the miserable monster whom I had created. He held up the curtain of the bed; and his eyes, if eyes they may be called, were fixed on me. His jaws opened, and he muttered some inarticulate sounds, while a grin wrinkled his cheeks. He might have spoken, but I did not hear; one hand was stretched out, seemingly to detain me, but I escaped and rushed down stairs. I took refuge in the courtyard belonging to the house which I inhabited; where I remained during the rest of the night, walking up and down in the greatest agitation, listening attentively, catching and fearing each sound as if it were to announce the approach of the demoniacal corpse to which I had so miserably given life.

Oh! no mortal could support the horror of that **countenance**. A mummy again endued with animation could not be so hideous as that wretch. I had gazed on him while unfinished; he was ugly then, but when those muscles and joints were rendered capable of motion, it became a thing such as even **Dante** could not have conceived.

---

agitated cause to move violently
delineate describe in words
luxuriances healthy features
ardour eagerness
traversing walking to and fro
lassitude tiredness
Ingolstadt a city in Germany
countenance face
Dante an Italian poet who lived in the Middle Ages
and wrote a famous poem about Hell

Extract from Charles Darwin's autobiography

> In the 19th century, the scientist Charles Darwin developed his theory of evolution – one of the most important scientific breakthroughs of all time. The following extract is taken from Charles Darwin's autobiography, first published in 1887, where he describes how his interest in the natural world developed whilst at Cambridge University when he began to collect beetles.

But no pursuit at Cambridge was followed with nearly so much eagerness or gave me so much pleasure as collecting beetles. It was the mere passion for collecting, for I did not dissect them and rarely compared their external characters with published descriptions, but got them named anyhow. I will give a proof of my zeal: one day, on tearing off some old bark, I saw two rare beetles and seized one in each hand; then I saw a third and new kind, which I could not bear to lose, so that I popped the one which I held in my right hand into my mouth. Alas it ejected some intensely acrid fluid, which burnt my tongue so that I was forced to spit the beetle out, which was lost, as well as the third one.

I was very successful in collecting and invented two

new methods; I employed a labourer to scrape during the winter, moss off old trees and place [it] in a large bag, and likewise to collect the rubbish at the bottom of the barges in which reeds are brought from the fens, and thus I got some very rare species. No poet ever felt more delight at seeing his first poem published than I did at seeing in Stephen's *Illustrations of British Insects* the magic words, "captured by C. Darwin, Esq."

Extract from *The Invisible Man* by H. G. Wells

The author H. G. Wells wrote many science fiction stories including *The War of the Worlds* and *The Time Machine*. The following extract is taken from his novel *The Invisible Man*, first published in 1897. Here, the Invisible Man, a scientist called Griffin, is talking to his acquaintance Dr Kemp and describing his first experiments to turn things invisible.

"I will tell you, Kemp, sooner or later, all the complicated processes. We need not go into that now. For the most part, saving certain gaps I chose to remember, they are written in cypher in those books that tramp has hidden. We must hunt him down. We must get those books again. But the essential phase was to place the transparent object whose refractive index was to be lowered between two radiating centres of a sort of **ethereal** vibration, of which I will tell you more fully later. No, not those **Röntgen vibrations**—I don't know that these others of mine have been described. Yet they are obvious enough. I needed two little dynamos, and these I worked with a cheap gas engine. My first experiment was with a bit of white wool fabric. It was the strangest thing in the world to see it in the flicker of the flashes soft and white, and then to watch it fade like a wreath of smoke and vanish.

"I could scarcely believe I had done it. I put my hand into the emptiness, and there was the thing as solid as ever. I felt it awkwardly, and threw it on the floor. I had a little trouble finding it again.

"And then came a curious experience. I heard a miaow behind me, and turning, saw a lean white cat, very dirty, on the cistern cover outside the window. A thought came into my head. 'Everything ready for you,' I said, and went to the window, opened it, and called softly. She came in, purring—the poor beast was starving—and I gave her some milk. All my food was in a cupboard in the corner of the room. After that she went smelling round the room, evidently with the idea of making herself at home. The invisible rag upset her a bit; you should have seen her spit at it! But I made her comfortable on the pillow of my truckle-bed. And I gave her butter to get her to wash."

"And you processed her?"

"I processed her. But giving drugs to a cat is no joke, Kemp! And the process failed."

"Failed!"

"In two particulars. These were the claws and the pigment stuff, what is it?—at the back of the eye in a cat. You know?"

"*Tapetum.*"

"Yes, the *tapetum*. It didn't go. After I'd given the stuff to bleach the blood and done certain other things to her, I gave the beast opium, and put her and the pillow she was sleeping on, on the apparatus. And after all the rest had faded and vanished, there remained two little ghosts of her eyes."

"Odd!"

"I can't explain it. She was bandaged and clamped, of course—so I had her safe; but she woke while she was still misty, and miaowed dismally, and someone came knocking. It was an old woman from downstairs, who suspected me of vivisecting—a drink-sodden old creature, with only a white cat to care for in all the world. I whipped out some chloroform, applied it, and answered the door. 'Did I hear a cat?' she asked. 'My cat?' 'Not here,' said I, very politely. She was a little doubtful and tried to peer past me into the room; strange enough to her no doubt—bare walls, uncurtained windows, truckle-bed, with the gas engine vibrating, and the seethe of the radiant points, and that faint ghastly stinging of chloroform in the air. She had to be satisfied at last and went away again."

"How long did it take?" asked Kemp.

"Three or four hours—the cat. The bones and sinews and the fat were the last to go, and the tips of the coloured hairs. And, as I say, the back part of the eye, tough, **iridescent** stuff it is, wouldn't go at all.

185

"It was night outside long before the business was over, and nothing was to be seen but the dim eyes and the claws. I stopped the gas engine, felt for and stroked the beast, which was still insensible, and then, being tired, left it sleeping on the invisible pillow and went to bed. I found it hard to sleep. I lay awake thinking weak aimless stuff, going over the experiment over and over again, or dreaming feverishly of things growing misty and vanishing about me, until everything, the ground I stood on, vanished, and so I came to that sickly falling nightmare one gets. About two, the cat began miaowing about the room. I tried to hush it by talking to it, and then I decided to turn it out. I remember the shock I had when striking a light—there were just the round eyes shining green—and nothing round them. I would have given it milk, but I hadn't any. It wouldn't be quiet, it just sat down and miaowed at the door. I tried to catch it, with an idea of putting it out of the window, but it wouldn't be caught, it vanished. Then it began miaowing in different parts of the room. At last I opened the window and made a bustle. I suppose it went out at last. I never saw any more of it.

"Then—Heaven knows why—I fell thinking of my father's funeral again, and the dismal windy hillside, until the day had come. I found sleeping was hopeless, and, locking my door after me, wandered out into the morning streets."

"You don't mean to say there's an invisible cat at large!" said Kemp.

"If it hasn't been killed," said the Invisible Man. "Why not?"

"Why not?" said Kemp. "I didn't mean to interrupt."

"It's very probably been killed," said the Invisible Man. "It was alive four days after, I know, and down a grating in Great Titchfield Street; because I saw a crowd round the place, trying to see whence the miaowing came."

---

ethereal intangible
Röntgen vibrations X-rays
iridescent colourful

Exploration and adventure

The 19th century was an age of exploration and adventure. From the jungles of the Amazon to the fiery volcanoes of the Pacific, 19th-century explorers helped to map the globe. It was also the age of empire and in the late 19th century, European powers such as Great Britain, Germany, France and Belgium invaded and colonized large parts of Africa, taking control of this vast continent's natural resources and ruling over its inhabitants.

Exploration was not only the preserve of the professional adventurer. Christian missionaries set out to far-flung corners of the globe to 'civilize' the people they found there, whilst scientists and naturalists explored remote places, discovering new species and strange phenomena. The stories they brought back inspired tales of adventure from authors such as Robert Louis Stevenson and H. Rider Haggard.

In this section, the accounts of these 19th-century European travellers and the extracts from 19th-century fiction reflect the beliefs of the time in which they were written.

Extract from *Through the Dark Continent* by Henry Morton Stanley

> In the late 19th century, European countries colonized large parts of the African continent. Henry Morton Stanley was a journalist and explorer who in the 1870s set out on an expedition to trace the course of the Congo river in Central Africa to the sea. The following extract is taken from his account of the expedition *Through the Dark Continent*, first published in 1878. Here, he describes a confrontation with a group of African tribes-people as his expedition party travels down the river.

In these wild regions our mere presence excited the most furious passions of hate and murder, just as in shallow waters a deep vessel stirs up muddy sediments. It appeared to be a necessity, then why should we regret it? Could a man contend with the inevitable?

At 2 p.m., heralded by savage shouts from the wasp storm, which from some cause or other are unusually exultant, we emerge out of the shelter of the deeply wooded banks in presence of a vast **affluent**, nearly 2000 yards across at the mouth. As soon as we have fairly entered its waters, we see a great concourse of canoes hovering about some islets, which stud the middle of the stream. The canoe-men, standing up, give a loud shout as they discern us, and blow their horns louder than ever. We pull briskly on to gain the right bank, and come in view of the right branch of the affluent, when, looking upstream, we see a sight that sends the blood tingling through every nerve and fibre of the body, arouses not only our most lively interest, but also our most lively apprehensions – a flotilla of gigantic canoes bearing down upon us, which both in size and numbers utterly eclipse anything encountered **hitherto**! Instead of aiming for the right bank, we form in line, and keep straight down the river, the boat taking position behind. Yet after a moment's reflection, as I note the numbers of the savages, and the daring manner of the pursuit, and the desire of our canoes to abandon the steady compact line, I give the order to drop anchor. Four of our canoes affect not to listen, until I chase them, and threaten them with my guns. This compelled them to return to the line, which is formed of eleven double canoes, anchored 10 yards apart. The boat moves up to the front and takes position 50 yards above them. The shields are next lifted by the non-combatants, men, women, and children, in the bows, and along the outer lines, as well as astern, and from behind these, the muskets and rifles are aimed.

We have sufficient time to take a view of the mighty force bearing down on us, and to count the number of the war-vessels which have been collected from the Livingstone and its great affluent. There are fifty-four of them! A monster canoe leads the way, with two rows of upstanding paddles, forty men on a side, their bodies bending and swaying in unison as with a swelling **barbarous** chorus they drive her down towards us. In the bow, standing on what appears to be a platform, are ten prime young warriors, their heads [bright] with feathers of the parrot, crimson and grey: at the stern, eight men, with long paddles, whose tops are decorated with ivory balls, guide the monster vessel; and dancing up and down from stern to stern are ten men, who appear to be chiefs. All the paddles are headed with ivory balls, every head bears a feather crown, every arm shows gleaming white ivory armlets. From the bow of the canoe streams a thick fringe of the long white fibre of the **Hyphene palm**. The crashing sound of large drums, a hundred blasts from ivory horns, and a thrilling chant from two thousand human throats, do not tend to soothe our nerves or to increase our confidence. However, it is 'neck or nothing.' We have no time to pray, or to take sentimental looks at the savage world, or even breathe a sad farewell to it. So many other things have to be done speedily and well.

As the foremost canoe comes rushing down, and its consorts on either side beating the water into foam, and raising their jets of water with their sharp prows, I turn to take a last look at our people, and say to them:

"Boys, be firm as iron; wait until you see the first spear, and then take good aim. Don't fire all at once. Keep aiming until you are sure of your man. Don't think of running away, for only your guns can save you."

The monster canoe aims straight for my boat, as though it would run us down; but, when within fifty yards off, swerves aside, and, when nearly opposite, the warriors above the manned prow let fly their spears, and on either side there is a noise of rushing bodies. But every sound is soon lost in the ripping, cracking **musketry**. For five minutes we are so absorbed in firing that we take no note of anything else; but at the end of that time we are made aware that the enemy is reforming about 200 yards above us.

Our blood is up now. It is a murderous world, and we feel for the first time that we hate the filthy, vulturous ghouls who inhabit it.

---

affluent a stream or river that flows into a larger one
hitherto until now
barbarous primitive, savage
Hyphene palm a type of palm tree
musketry rifles

Extract from *Heart of Darkness* by Joseph Conrad

> In the following extract from the novel *Heart of Darkness*, first published in 1899, the narrator describes his experience of travelling down the Congo River in Central Africa.

"Going up that river was like travelling back to the earliest beginnings of the world, when vegetation rioted on the earth and the big trees were kings. An empty stream, a great silence, an impenetrable forest. The air was warm, thick, heavy, sluggish. There was no joy in the brilliance of sunshine. The long stretches of the waterway ran on, deserted, into the gloom of overshadowed distances. On silvery sandbanks hippos and alligators sunned themselves side by side. The broadening waters flowed through a mob of wooded islands; you lost your way on that river as you would in a desert, and butted all day long against shoals, trying to find the channel, till you thought yourself bewitched and cut off for ever from everything you had known once—somewhere—far away—in another existence perhaps. There were moments when one's past came back to one, as it will sometimes when you have not a moment to spare to yourself; but it came in the shape of an unrestful and noisy dream, remembered with wonder amongst the overwhelming realities of this strange world of plants, and water, and silence. And this stillness of life did not in the least resemble a peace. It was the stillness of an **implacable** force brooding over an **inscrutable** intention. It looked at you with a vengeful aspect. I got used to it afterwards; I did not see it any more; I had no time. I had to keep guessing at the channel; I had to discern, mostly by inspiration, the signs of hidden banks; I watched for sunken stones; I was learning to clap my teeth smartly before my heart flew out, when I shaved by a fluke some infernal sly old snag that would have ripped the life out of the tin-pot steamboat and drowned all the pilgrims; I had to keep a look-out for the signs of dead wood we could cut up in the night for next day's steaming. When you have to attend to things of that sort, to the mere incidents of the surface, the reality—the reality, I tell you—fades. The inner truth is hidden—luckily, luckily. But I felt it all the same; I felt often its mysterious stillness watching me at my monkey tricks.

Sometimes we came upon a station close by the bank, clinging to the skirts of the unknown, and the white men rushing out of a tumble-down hovel, with great gestures of joy and surprise and welcome, seemed very strange,—

had the appearance of being held there captive by a spell. The word ivory would ring in the air for a while— and on we went again into the silence, along empty reaches, round the still bends, between the high walls of our winding way, reverberating in hollow claps the ponderous beat of the stern-wheel. Trees, trees, millions of trees, massive, immense, running up high; and at their foot, hugging the bank against the stream, crept the little begrimed steamboat, like a sluggish beetle crawling on the floor of a lofty **portico**. It made you feel very small, very lost, and yet it was not altogether depressing, that feeling. After all, if you were small, the grimy beetle crawled on—which was just what you wanted it to do. The reaches opened before us and closed behind, as if the forest had stepped leisurely across the water to bar the way for our return. We penetrated deeper and deeper into the heart of darkness. It was very quiet there. At night sometimes the roll of drums behind the curtain of trees would run up the river and remain sustained faintly, as if hovering in the air high over our heads, till the first break of day. Whether it meant war, peace, or prayer we could not tell.

---

implacable impossible to appease
inscrutable hard to understand
portico porch or covered walkway

Extract from *On Sledge and Horseback to Outcast Siberian Lepers* by Kate Marsden

Kate Marsden was a British missionary and explorer who in 1891 set out on an expedition to Siberia to try to find a cure for leprosy. The following extract is taken from her account of this expedition, *On Sledge and Horseback to Outcast Siberian Lepers*, first published in 1893. Here, she describes her journey through mosquito-infested marshes and forests.

More bogs and marshes for several miles; and then I grew so sleepy and sick that I begged to rest, notwithstanding our position on semi-marshy ground, which had not as yet dried from the heat of the summer sun. I was asleep in five minutes, lying on the damp ground with only a fan to shelter me from the sun.

On again for a few more miles; but I began to feel the effects of this sort of travelling – in a word, I felt utterly worn out. It was as much as I could do to hold on to the horse, and I nearly tumbled off several times in the effort. The cramp in my body and lower limbs was indescribable, and I had to discard the cushion under me, because it became soaked through and through with the rain, and rode on the broad, bare, wooden saddle. What feelings of relief arose when the time of rest came, and the pitching of tents, and the brewing of tea! Often I slept quite soundly till morning, awaking to find that the mosquitoes had been hard at work in my slumbers, in spite of veil and gloves, leaving great itching lumps, that turned me sick. Once we saw two calves that had died from exhaustion from the bites of these pests, and the white hair of our poor horses was generally covered with clots of blood, due partly to mosquitoes and partly to prodigious horse-flies. But those lepers – they suffered far more than I suffered, and that was the one thought, added to the strength that God supplied, that kept me from collapsing entirely.

My second thunderstorm was far worse than the first, The forest seemed on fire, and the rain dashed in our faces with almost blinding force. My horse plunged and reared, flew first to one side, and then to the other, dragging me amongst bushes and trees, so that I was in danger of being caught by the branches and hurled to the ground. After this storm one of the horses, carrying stores and other things, sank into a bog nearly to its neck; and the help of all the men was required to get it out.

Soon after the storm we were camping and drinking tea, when I noticed that all the men were eagerly talking together and gesticulating. I asked what it all meant, and was told that a large bear was supposed to be in the neighbourhood, according to a report from a post-station close at hand. There was a general priming of fire-arms, except in my case, for I did not know how to use my revolver, so thought I had better pass it on to someone else, lest I might shoot a man in mistake for a bear. We mounted again and went on. The usual chattering this time was exchanged for a dead silence, this being our first bear experience; but we grew wiser as we proceeded, and substituted noise for silence. We hurried on, as fast as possible, to get through the miles of forests and bogs. I found it best not to look about me, because, when I did so, every large stump of a fallen tree took the shape of a bear. When my horse stumbled over the roots of a tree, or shied at some object unseen by me, my heart began to gallop.

Extract from *Treasure Island* by Robert Louis Stevenson

FICTION

> The following extract is taken from the novel *Treasure Island*, which was first published in 1883. Here, after landing on the desert island of the title, Jim Hawkins, a cabin boy, has fled from Long John Silver who has led a mutiny against the captain of their ship.

I was so pleased at having given the slip to Long John that I began to enjoy myself and look around me with some interest on the strange land that I was in.

I had crossed a marshy tract full of willows, bulrushes, and odd, outlandish, swampy trees; and I had now come out upon the skirts of an open piece of undulating, sandy country, about a mile long, dotted with a few pines and a great number of contorted trees, not unlike the oak in growth, but pale in the foliage, like willows. On the far side of the open stood one of the hills, with two quaint, craggy peaks shining vividly in the sun.

I now felt for the first time the joy of exploration. The isle was uninhabited; my shipmates I had left behind, and nothing lived in front of me but dumb brutes and fowls. I turned hither and thither among the trees. Here and there were flowering plants, unknown to me; here and there I saw snakes, and one raised his head from a ledge of rock and hissed at me with a noise not unlike the spinning of a top. Little did I suppose that he was a deadly enemy and that the noise was the famous rattle.

Then I came to a long thicket of these oaklike trees— live, or evergreen, oaks, I heard afterwards they should be called—which grew low along the sand like brambles, the boughs curiously twisted, the foliage compact, like thatch. The thicket stretched down from the top of one of the sandy knolls, spreading and growing taller as it went, until it reached the margin of the broad, reedy fen, through which the nearest of the little rivers soaked its way into the anchorage. The marsh was steaming in the strong sun, and the outline of the Spy-glass trembled through the haze.

All at once there began to go a sort of bustle among the bulrushes; a wild duck flew up with a quack, another followed, and soon over the whole surface of the marsh a great cloud of birds hung screaming and circling in the air. I judged at once that some of my shipmates must be drawing near along the borders of the fen. Nor was I deceived, for soon I heard the very distant and low tones of a human voice, which, as I continued to give ear, grew steadily louder and nearer.

This put me in a great fear, and I crawled under cover of the nearest live-oak and squatted there, **hearkening**, as silent as a mouse.

Another voice answered, and then the first voice, which

I now recognized to be Silver's, once more took up the story and ran on for a long while in a stream, only now and again interrupted by the other. By the sound they must have been talking earnestly, and almost fiercely; but no distinct word came to my hearing.

At last the speakers seemed to have paused and perhaps to have sat down, for not only did they cease to draw any nearer, but the birds themselves began to grow more quiet and to settle again to their places in the swamp.

And now I began to feel that I was neglecting my business, that since I had been so foolhardy as to come ashore with these desperadoes, the least I could do was to overhear them at their councils, and that my plain and obvious duty was to draw as close as I could manage, under the favourable ambush of the crouching trees.

I could tell the direction of the speakers pretty exactly, not only by the sound of their voices but by the behaviour of the few birds that still hung in alarm above the heads of the intruders.

Crawling on all fours, I made steadily but slowly towards them, till at last, raising my head to an **aperture** among the leaves, I could see clear down into a little green dell beside the marsh, and closely set about with trees, where Long John Silver and another of the crew stood face to face in conversation.

---

hearkening listening
aperture opening

Extract from *The Naturalist on the River Amazons* by Henry Bates

> Henry Bates was a 19th-century naturalist who travelled to the Amazon in South America to study the wildlife there. The following extract is taken from his book *The Naturalist on the River Amazons*, which was first published in 1863. Here, he describes the sounds of the Amazon forest and the local people's belief in the Curupíra or wild man of the forest.

We often read, in books of travels, of the silence and gloom of the Brazilian forests. They are realities, and the impression deepens on a longer acquaintance. The few sounds of birds are of that pensive or mysterious character which intensifies the feeling of solitude rather than imparts a sense of life and cheerfulness. Sometimes, in the midst of the stillness, a sudden yell or scream will startle one; this comes from some defenceless fruit-eating animal, which is pounced upon by a tiger-cat or stealthy boa-constrictor. Morning and evening the howling monkeys make a most fearful and harrowing noise, under which it is difficult to keep up one's buoyancy of spirit.

The feeling of inhospitable wildness which the forest is calculated to inspire, is increased tenfold under this fearful uproar. Often, even in the still hours of midday, a sudden crash will be heard resounding afar through the wilderness, as some great bough or entire tree falls to the ground. There are, besides, many sounds which it is impossible to account for. I found the natives generally as much at a loss in this respect as myself. Sometimes a sound is heard like the clang of an iron bar against a hard, hollow tree, or a piercing cry rends the air; these are not repeated, and the succeeding silence tends to heighten the unpleasant impression which they make on the mind. With the native it is always the Curupíra, the wild man or spirit of the forest, which produces all noises they are unable to explain. For myths are the rude theories which mankind, in the infancy of knowledge, invent to explain natural phenomena. The Curupíra is a mysterious being, whose attributes are uncertain, for they vary according to locality. Sometimes he is described as a kind of orang-otang, being covered with long, shaggy hair, and living in trees. At others he is said to have cloven feet, and a bright red face. He has a wife and children, and sometimes comes down to the **rocas** to steal the **mandioca**.

---

rocas rocks
mandioca an edible plant

Extract from *She* by H. Rider Haggard

> The following extract is taken from the novel *She*,
> which was first published in 1887. This adventure story
> describes the journey of Horace Holly, Leo Vincey and
> their servant, Job, to a remote, lost African kingdom.
> Here, the three men are camping at night by the edge of a
> lake with lions prowling on the opposite bank.

I do not quite know what it was that made me poke my
head out of the friendly shelter of the blanket, perhaps
because I found that the mosquitoes were biting right
through it. Anyhow, as I did so I heard Job whisper, in a
frightened voice—

"Oh, my stars, look there!"

Instantly we all of us looked, and this was what we
saw in the moonlight. Near the shore were two wide and
ever-widening circles of concentric rings rippling away
across the surface of the water, and in the heart and centre
of the circles were two dark moving objects.

"What is it?" asked I.

"It is those damned lions, sir," answered Job, in a tone
which was an odd mixture of a sense of personal injury,
habitual respect, and acknowledged fear, "and they are

swimming here to *heat* us," he added, nervously picking up an "h" in his agitation.

I looked again: there was no doubt about it; I could catch the glare of their ferocious eyes. Attracted either by the smell of the newly killed waterbuck meat or of ourselves, the hungry beasts were actually storming our position.

Leo already had his rifle in his hand. I called to him to wait till they were nearer, and meanwhile grabbed my own. Some fifteen feet from us the water shallowed on a bank to the depth of about fifteen inches, and presently the first of them—it was the lioness—got on to it, shook herself, and roared. At that moment Leo fired, the bullet went right down her open mouth and out at the back of her neck, and down she dropped, with a splash, dead. The other lion—a full-grown male—was some two paces behind her. At this second he got his forepaws on to the bank, when a strange thing happened. There was a rush and disturbance of the water, such as one sees in a pond in England when a pike takes a little fish, only a thousand times fiercer and larger, and suddenly the lion gave a most terrific snarling roar and sprang forward on to the bank, dragging something black with him.

"Allah!" shouted Mahomed, "a crocodile has got him by the leg!" and sure enough he had. We could see the long snout with its gleaming lines of teeth and the reptile body behind it.

And then followed an extraordinary scene indeed. The lion managed to get well on to the bank, the crocodile half standing and half swimming, still nipping his hind leg. He roared till the air quivered with the sound, and then, with a savage, shrieking snarl, turned round and clawed hold of the crocodile's head. The crocodile shifted his grip, having, as we afterwards discovered, had one of his eyes torn out, and slightly turned over; instantly the lion got him by the throat and held on, and then over and over they rolled upon the bank struggling hideously. It was impossible to follow their movements, but when next we got a clear view the tables had turned, for the crocodile, whose head seemed to be a mass of gore, had got the lion's body in his iron jaws just above the hips, and was squeezing him and shaking him to and fro. For his part, the tortured brute, roaring in agony, was clawing and biting madly at his enemy's scaly head, and fixing his great hind claws in the crocodile's, comparatively speaking, soft throat, ripping it open as one would rip a glove.

Then, all of a sudden, the end came. The lion's head fell forward on the crocodile's back, and with an awful groan he died, and the crocodile, after standing for a minute motionless, slowly rolled over on to his side, his jaws still fixed across the carcase of the lion, which, we afterwards found, he had bitten almost in halves.

Extract from *The Hawaiian Archipelago* by Isabella Bird

> Isabella Bird was a Victorian explorer who travelled
> extensively in America, Australasia and Asia. The
> following extract is taken from her book *The Hawaiian
> Archipelago*, which was first published in 1875. Here she
> describes a visit she made to Kilauea, an active volcano
> in Hawaii.

I have no room in my thoughts for anything but volcanoes,
and it will be so for some days to come. We have been all
day in the crater, in fact, I left Mr. Green and his native
there, and came up with the guide, sore, stiff, bruised,
cut, singed, grimy, with my thick gloves shrivelled off
by the touch of sulphurous acid, and my boots nearly
burned off. But what are cuts, bruises, fatigue, and singed
eyelashes, in comparison with the awful **sublimities** I have
witnessed today? The activity of Kilauea on Jan. 31 was as
child's play to its activity today: as a display of fireworks
compared to the conflagration of a metropolis. *Then*, the
sense of awe gave way speedily to that of admiration of
the dancing fire fountains of a fiery lake; *now*, it was all
terror, horror, and sublimity, blackness, suffocating gases,
scorching heat, crashings, surgings, detonations; half-seen

fires, hideous, tortured, wallowing waves. I feel as if the terrors of Kilauea would haunt me all my life, and be the **Nemesis** of weak and tired hours.

The whole region vibrated with the shock of the fiery surges. To stand there was "to snatch a fearful joy," out of a pain and terror which were unendurable. For two or three minutes we kept going to the edge, seeing the spectacle as with a flash, through half-closed eyes, and going back again; but a few trials, in which throats, nostrils, and eyes were irritated to torture by the acid gases, convinced us that it was unsafe to attempt to remain by the lake, as the pain and gasping for breath which followed each inhalation, threatened serious consequences.

With regard to the north lake we were more fortunate, and more persevering, and I regard the three hours we spent by it as containing some of the most solemn, as well as most fascinating, experiences of my life. The aspect of the volcano had altogether changed within four months. At present there are two lakes surrounded by precipices about eighty feet high. Owing to the smoke and confusion, it is most difficult to estimate their size even approximately, but I think that the diameter of the two cannot be less than a fifth of a mile.

Within the pit or lake by which we spent the morning, there were no fiery fountains, or regular **plashings** of fiery waves playing in indescribable beauty in a faint blue atmosphere, but lurid, gory, molten, raging, sulphurous, tormented masses of matter, half-seen through masses as restless, of lurid smoke. Apparently, huge bulging masses of a lurid-coloured lava were wallowing the whole time one over another in a central whirlpool, which occasionally flung up a wave of fire thirty or forty feet. The greatest intensity of action was always preceded by a dull throbbing roar, as if the imprisoned gases were seeking the vent which was afforded them by the upward bulging of the wave and its bursting into spray. The colour of the lava which appeared to be thrown upwards from great depths was more fiery and less gory than that nearer the surface. Now and then, through rifts in the smoke we saw a convergence of the whole molten mass into the centre, which rose wallowing and convulsed to a considerable height. The awful sublimity of what we did see, was enhanced by the knowledge that it was only a thousandth part of what we did not see, mere momentary glimpses of a terror and fearfulness which otherwise could not have been borne.

A ledge, only three or four feet wide, hung over the lake, and between that and the comparative *terra firma* of the older lava, there was a fissure of unknown depth, emitting hot blasts of **pernicious** gases. The guide would not venture on the outside ledge, but Mr. Green, in his scientific zeal, crossed the crack, telling me not to follow him, but presently, in his absorption with what he saw, called to me to come, and I jumped across, and this remained our perilous standpoint.

Burned, singed, stifled, blinded, only able to stand on one foot at a time, jumping back across the fissure every two or three minutes to escape an unendurable whiff of heat and sulphurous stench, or when splitting sounds below threatened the disruption of the ledge, lured as often back by the fascination of the horrors below; so we spent three hours.

There was every circumstance of awfulness to make the impression of the sight indelible. Sometimes dense volumes of smoke hid everything, and yet, upwards, from out "their sulphurous canopy" fearful sounds rose, crashings, thunderings, detonations, and we never knew then whether the spray of some hugely uplifted wave might not dash up to where we stood. At other times the smoke partially lifting, but still swirling in strong eddies, revealed a central whirlpool of fire, wallowing at unknown depths, to which the lava, from all parts of the lake, slid centrewards and downwards as into a vortex, where it mingled its waves with indescribable noise and fury, and then, breaking upwards, dashed itself to a great height in fierce, gory gouts and clots, while hell itself seemed opening at our feet.

---

sublimities powerful sights
Nemesis enemy
plashings light splashes
pernicious harmful

Death and disease

Death stalked the streets of 19th-century Britain. With overcrowded houses, poor sanitation and overflowing cemeteries, the rapidly growing towns and cities were breeding grounds for deadly diseases. For every hundred babies born in the last decade of the 19th century, fifteen of these children would not survive past their first birthday. Overseas conflicts such as the Crimean War claimed the lives of thousands of British soldiers, with the majority of fatalities the result of disease and injury rather than death on the battlefield.

With death so close at hand, many Victorians held a strong belief in the supernatural. Spiritualists who claimed to be able to communicate with the dead drew large crowds whilst others attempted to expose these mediums as frauds. Ghost stories filled the pages of books and magazines with 19th-century readers thrilled by tales of terror from authors such as Charles Dickens and M. R. James.

Medicine advertisement

To ward off sickness and disease, the Victorians placed their faith in a variety of treatments and medicines. Here is an advertisement for medicine published in 1891 in *Pick Me Up* magazine.

"FOR THE BLOOD IS THE LIFE"

CLARKE'S

WORLD-FAMED

BLOOD MIXTURE

Is warranted to cleanse the blood from all impurities from *whatever* cause arising. For Scrofula, Scurvy, Eczema, Skin and Blood Diseases, Pimples and Sores of all kinds, its effects are marvellous. It is the only real specific for Gout and Rheumatic Pains, for it removes the *cause* from the blood and bones. Thousands of Testimonials. In bottles 2s. 9d. and 11s. each, of all Chemists. Sent for 33 or 132 stamps, by Proprietors. Lincoln & Midland Counties Drug Co., Lincoln.
BEWARE OF WORTHLESS IMITATIONS.

Extract from *The Picture of Dorian Gray* by Oscar Wilde

The following extract is taken from the novel *The Picture of Dorian Gray*, first published in 1891. In this novel, a handsome man named Dorian Gray has his portrait painted and, fearing that his beauty will fade over time, sells his soul to ensure that whilst he stays forever youthful his portrait will age and fade instead. Here, Dorian reveals the hideous portrait to his friend, Basil Hallward, the artist who painted it originally.

He passed out of the room and began the ascent, Basil Hallward following close behind. They walked softly, as men do instinctively at night. The lamp cast fantastic shadows on the wall and staircase. A rising wind made some of the windows rattle.

When they reached the top landing, Dorian set the lamp down on the floor, and taking out the key, turned it in the lock. "You insist on knowing, Basil?" he asked in a low voice.

"Yes."

"I am delighted," he answered, smiling. Then he added, somewhat harshly, "You are the one man in the world who is entitled to know everything about me. You have had more to do with my life than you think"; and, taking up the lamp, he opened the door and went in. A cold current of air passed them, and the light shot up for a moment in a flame of murky orange. He shuddered. "Shut the door behind you," he whispered, as he placed the lamp on the table.

Hallward glanced round him with a puzzled expression. The room looked as if it had not been lived in for years. A faded Flemish tapestry, a curtained picture, an old Italian *cassone*, and an almost empty book-case—that was all that it seemed to contain, besides a chair and a table. As Dorian Gray was lighting a half-burned candle that was standing on the mantelshelf, he saw that the whole place was covered with dust and that the carpet was in holes. A mouse ran scuffling behind the wainscoting. There was a damp odour of mildew.

"So you think that it is only God who sees the soul, Basil? Draw that curtain back, and you will see mine."

The voice that spoke was cold and cruel. "You are mad, Dorian, or playing a part," muttered Hallward, frowning.

"You won't? Then I must do it myself," said the young man, and he tore the curtain from its rod and flung it on the ground.

An exclamation of horror broke from the painter's lips as he saw in the dim light the hideous face on the canvas grinning at him. There was something in its expression

214

that filled him with disgust and loathing. Good heavens! it was Dorian Gray's own face that he was looking at! The horror, whatever it was, had not yet entirely spoiled that marvellous beauty. There was still some gold in the thinning hair and some scarlet on the sensual mouth. The sodden eyes had kept something of the loveliness of their blue, the noble curves had not yet completely passed away from chiselled nostrils and from plastic throat. Yes, it was Dorian himself. But who had done it? He seemed to recognize his own brushwork, and the frame was his own design. The idea was monstrous, yet he felt afraid. He seized the lighted candle, and held it to the picture. In the left-hand corner was his own name, traced in long letters of bright vermilion.

It was some foul parody, some infamous **ignoble** satire. He had never done that. Still, it was his own picture. He knew it, and he felt as if his blood had changed in a moment from fire to sluggish ice. His own picture! What did it mean? Why had it altered? He turned and looked at Dorian Gray with the eyes of a sick man. His mouth twitched, and his parched tongue seemed unable to articulate. He passed his hand across his forehead. It was dank with clammy sweat.

The young man was leaning against the mantelshelf, watching him with that strange expression that one sees on the faces of those who are absorbed in a play when some great artist is acting. There was neither real sorrow in it nor real joy. There was simply the passion of the spectator, with perhaps a flicker of triumph in his eyes. He had taken the flower out of his coat, and was smelling it, or pretending to do so.

"What does this mean?" cried Hallward, at last. His own voice sounded shrill and curious in his ears.

"Years ago, when I was a boy," said Dorian Gray, crushing the flower in his hand, "you met me, flattered me, and taught me to be vain of my good looks. One day you introduced me to a friend of yours, who explained to me the wonder of youth, and you finished a portrait of me that revealed to me the wonder of beauty. In a mad moment that, even now, I don't know whether I regret or not, I made a wish, perhaps you would call it a prayer...."

"I remember it! Oh, how well I remember it! No! the thing is impossible. The room is damp. Mildew has got into the canvas. The paints I used had some wretched mineral poison in them. I tell you the thing is impossible."

"Ah, what is impossible?" murmured the young man, going over to the window and leaning his forehead against the cold, mist-stained glass.

"You told me you had destroyed it."

"I was wrong. It has destroyed me."

---

cassone an ornamental chest
ignoble dishonourable

Extract from Mary Seacole's autobiography

> Between 1853 and 1856, the Crimean War fought between the Russian Empire and an alliance of the United Kingdom, France and other nations claimed many lives. Mary Seacole was a nurse who travelled to the Crimea to help the wounded soldiers there. The following extract is taken from her autobiography, which was first published in 1858, and describes her experience of the battle of the Tchernaya, which was fought on 16th August 1855.

It was a fearful scene; but why repeat this remark. All death is trying to witness—even that of the good man who lays down his life hopefully and peacefully; but on the battle-field, when the poor body is torn and rent in hideous ways, and the scared spirit struggles to loose itself from the still strong frame that holds it tightly to the last, death is fearful indeed. It had come peacefully enough to some. They lay with half-opened eyes, and a quiet smile about the lips that showed their end to have been painless; others it had arrested in the heat of passion, and frozen on their **pallid** faces a glare of hatred and defiance that made your warm blood run cold. But little time had we to think of the dead, whose business it was to see after the dying, who might yet be saved. The ground was thickly **cumbered** with the wounded, some of them calm and resigned, others impatient and restless, a few filling the air with their cries of pain—all wanting water, and grateful to those who administered it, and more substantial comforts.

I attended to the wounds of many French and Sardinians, and helped to lift them into the ambulances, which came tearing up to the scene of action. I derived no little gratification from being able to dress the wounds of several Russians; indeed, they were as kindly treated as the others. One of them was badly shot in the lower jaw, and was beyond my or any human skill. Incautiously I inserted my finger into his mouth to feel where the ball had lodged, and his teeth closed upon it, in the agonies of death, so tightly that I had to call to those around to release it, which was not done until it had been bitten so deeply that I shall carry the scar with me to my grave. Poor fellow, he meant me no harm, for, as the near approach of death softened his features, a smile spread over his rough inexpressive face, and so he died.

I attended another Russian, a handsome fellow, and an officer, shot in the side, who bore his cruel suffering with a firmness that was very noble. In return for the little use I was to him, he took a ring off his finger and gave it to me, and after I had helped to lift him into the ambulance he kissed my hand and smiled far more thanks than I had earned. I do not know whether he survived his wounds, but I fear not. Many others, on that day, gave me thanks in words the meaning of which was lost upon me, and all of them in that one common language of the whole world—smiles.

I picked up some trophies from the battle-field, but not many, and those of little value. I cannot bear the idea of plundering either the living or the dead; but I picked up a Russian metal cross, and took from the bodies of some of the poor fellows nothing of more value than a few buttons, which I severed from their coarse grey coats.

So end my reminiscences of the battle of the Tchernaya, fought, as all the world knows, on the 16th of August, 1855.

pallid pale
cumbered littered, cluttered

Extract from *The Mysteries of London* by G. W. M. Reynolds

FICTION

> As the population of London grew in the 19th century, the city's cemeteries became increasingly overcrowded. The following extract is taken from *The Mysteries of London*, a popular 'penny dreadful' published in 1845. Here, the author describes how one grave-digger makes room for a new burial in the cemetery he works in.

The grave-digger entered the cemetery, and cast a glance around him.

That glance well expressed the man's thoughts; for he mentally asked himself, "Whose grave must I disturb now to make room for the new one?"

At length he advanced towards a particular spot, considered it for a moment, and then struck his spade into the soil, as much as to say, "This will do."

The place where he had now halted was only a few yards from the Bone-House. Taking a key from his pocket, he proceeded to unlock the door of that building.

Entering the Bone-House he took from amongst a quantity of implements in one corner, a long flexible iron rod similar to those which we have already described as being used by the **body-snatchers**.

Returning to the grave, he thrust the rod into the ground. It met with a little resistance from some substance a little harder than the soil; but the man pushed it downwards with a strong arm; and it sank at least twelve feet into the ground.

Satisfied with this essay of the nature of the spot, the grave-digger drew back the rod; and from the deep but narrow aperture thus formed, issued a stench more **pestiferous** than that which ever came from the lowest knacker's yard.

The man retreated rapidly to the Bone-House; that odour was too powerful even for one who had passed the greater portion of his life in that very grave-yard.

He now proceeded to light a fire in the Bone-House; and when he saw the huge logs which he heaped on the grate, blazing brightly, he covered them with coke. The current of air from the open door fanned the flames, which roared up the chimney; and the grave-digger felt invigorated and cheered by the genial warmth that issued from the ample grate.

After lingering for a few minutes in the Bone House, the grave-digger returned to the spot which he had previously marked for excavation.

Baring his brawny arms to the very shoulders, he now set himself vigorously to work to dig the grave which was to receive a newcomer that afternoon.

Throwing the earth up on either side, he had digged to

a depth of about two feet, when his spade encountered a coffin. He immediately took his pickaxe, broke the coffin to pieces, and then separated with his shovel the pieces of wood and the human bones from the damp earth. The coffin was already so soft with decay that the iron rod had penetrated through it without much difficulty; and it therefore required but little exertion to break it up altogether.

But the odour which came from the grave was now of the most nauseating kind – **fetid**, sickly, pestiferous – making the atmosphere heavy, and the human breath thick and clammy, as it were – and causing even that experienced grave-digger to retch as if he were about to vomit.

Leaping from the grave, he began to busy himself in conveying the pieces of the broken coffin and the putrid remains of mortality into the Bone-House, where he heaped them pell-mell upon the fire.

The flesh had not completely decayed all away from the bones; a thick, black, fatty-looking substance still covered those human relics; and the fire was thus fed with a material which made the flames roar and play half up the chimney.

The man returned to the grave, and was about to resume his labour, when his eyes caught sight of a black object, almost embedded in the damp clay heaped up by the side. He turned it over with his spade: it was the upper part of the skull, with the long, dark hair of a woman still remaining attached to it. The grave-digger coolly took up the relic by that long hair which perhaps had once been a valued ornament; and, carrying it in this manner into the Bone-House, threw it upon the fire. The hair hissed for a moment as it burnt, for it was damp and clogged with clay; then the voracious flames licked up the thin coat of blackened flesh which had still remained on the skull; and lastly devoured the bone itself.

The grave-digger returned to his toils; and at a depth of scarcely one foot below the coffin thus exhumed and burnt, his shovel was again impeded for a moment – and by another coffin!

Once more was the pickaxe put into requisition a second coffin was broken up; another decomposing, but not entirely decomposed, corpse was hacked, and hewed, and rent to pieces by the merciless implement which was wielded by a merciless arm;- and in a few moments, the fire in the Bone-House burnt cheerfully once more, the mouth of the chimney vomiting forth its dense and pest-bearing breath, the volume of which was from time to time lighted with sparks and flakes of fire.

Thus was it that this grave-digger disposed of the old tenants of the cemetery in order to make room for new ones.

---

body-snatchers grave-robbers
pestiferous infected with a deadly disease
fetid decaying smell

Extract from *The Bristol Mercury* newspaper

In the 19th century, spiritualists and mediums claimed they could communicate with the spirits of the dead. Table-rapping or spirit-rapping – where the sounds of knocking or tapping would be made without any apparent human intervention – was one of the ways in which it was claimed the dead could communicate with the living. Some people attempted to disprove this and the following extract is taken from a newspaper report published in *The Bristol Mercury* on 4th August 1855. The report describes how Professor Anderson, a magician also known as the Great Wizard of the North, who claimed that 'spirit-rapping' was a fraud, was visited by a man and his daughter who claimed that they could prove that it was true. Here, the man and his daughter demonstrate 'spirit-rapping' to Professor Anderson and claim to make contact with a spirit called Mary Jemima.

"She is here!" cried the man. "Are you there, Mary Jemima?"

"Who is Mary Jemima?" asked Mr Anderson.

"It is my first wife – that was her name," replied the man.

A knock by the table was the answer that Mary Jemima was in attendance. Another knock announced that she was willing to be interrogated on any subject. Various questions were addressed to her through the medium of the girl. The replies were given by the table tilting over and striking the floor with one of its legs. A knock was understood to be an affirmative reply to the question, while no knock was understood to be an answer in the negative. Nothing could be more evident that the motion of the table resulted from the pressure of the girl's fingers on its circumference. To prove this, Mr Anderson suggested that some soot should be spread on it, by the adhesion of which to the girl's fingers her pressure on the table would be detected. This was done; but on Mary Jemima being now asked a question there was no reply. "She is offended at being doubted by you," said the man. "Her spirit does not like to be trifled with." "Very well," rejoined Mr Anderson, "the interview has been most interesting. Would you be so good to come to the Music-hall this evening? I am performing there, and I should like you to try the table before the audience." The man assented: the evening came. After the wizard had worked many of his wonders, the rapping-table was introduced. Mr Anderson made his own comments on the spirit-rappers, and then introduced his visitors of the morning; telling the people that he thought he had as much command over the spirit of "Mary Jemima" as her former husband had. The *media* took their places at the table; the audience were silent; "Mary Jemima" was called, and answered. Mr Anderson put the first question through the medium.

"Are you happier than you were when on earth with your husband?" he asked. The table replied in the affirmative.

"Do you think him to be a wise and good man?" There was an ominous silence, implying that the spirit did not think so.

"Do you consider spirit-rapping to be a juggle and a deceit?" The table replied "yes" to the astonishment of the audience and the operators.

"Do you consider your former husband to be a gross imposter?" The answer was again "yes." The audience laughed uproariously.

Mr Anderson proceeded. "Do you think he ought to be respected?" No answer. "Do you think he ought to be kicked out?" "Yes, yes," rapped the table more vigorously than ever.

The man and the girl sprang to their feet. "This is not my Mary Jemima – it is an evil spirit. Unloose me – unhand me, Satan!" he cried as he struggled across the platform, dragging the table with him, which seemed firmly glued to his finger-ends, the audience all the while being convulsed with merriment.

"Stop!" cried Mr Anderson, "Mary Jemima will obey me better than she will you. I have her here in the wire of this **galvanic** battery. I detach the wire, and you are free. Go home in peace, and meddle not with the spirits again."

The man looked savagely at the table, and lifted up his foot to kick it in his anger. In an instant it sprang up, and rolled over his feet.

"Oh, my corns – my corns!" he cried, as, limping from the platform, he left the Hall, amidst the derisive shouts of the company.

galvanic electrical

Extract from *Lost Hearts*
by M. R. James

Ghost stories were very popular in the Victorian era. The
following extract is taken from the short story *Lost Hearts*,
which was first published in 1895. In this story, a young
boy called Stephen Abney has been invited by his older
cousin, Mr Abney, to stay at his home, Aswarby Hall.
Here, Stephen is looking out of his bedroom window at
night as he waits to meet his uncle in his study at 11pm.

The wind had fallen, and there was a still night and a
full moon. At about ten o'clock Stephen was standing at
the open window of his bedroom, looking out over the
country. Still as the night was, the mysterious population
of the distant moonlit woods was not yet lulled to rest.

From time to time strange cries as of lost and despairing
wanderers sounded from across the mere. They might be
the notes of owls or water-birds, yet they did not quite
resemble either sound.

Were not they coming nearer? Now they sounded
from the nearer side of the water, and in a few moments
they seemed to be floating about among the shrubberies.

Then they ceased. But just as Stephen was thinking
of shutting the window and resuming his reading of

Robinson Crusoe, he caught sight of two figures standing on the gravelled terrace that ran along the garden side of the Hall — the figures of a boy and girl, as it seemed; they stood side by side, looking up at the windows.

Something in the form of the girl recalled irresistibly his dream of the figure in the bath. The boy inspired him with more acute fear.

Whilst the girl stood still, half-smiling, with her hands clasped over her heart, the boy, a thin shape, with black hair and ragged clothing, raised his arms in the air with an appearance of menace and of unappeasable hunger and longing.

The moon shone upon his almost transparent hands, and Stephen saw that the nails were fearfully long and that the light shone through them.

As he stood with his arms thus raised, he disclosed a terrifying spectacle. On the left side of his chest there opened a black and gaping rent, and there fell upon Stephen's brain, rather than upon his ear, the impression of one of those hungry and desolate cries that he had heard resounding over the woods of Aswarby all that evening.

In another moment this dreadful pair had moved swiftly and noiselessly over the dry gravel, and he saw them no more.

Inexpressibly frightened as he was, he determined to take his candle and go down to Mr Abney's study, for the hour appointed for their meeting was near at hand.

The study or library opened out of the front hall on one side, and Stephen, urged on by his terrors, did not take long in getting there.

To effect an entrance was not so easy. The door was not locked, he felt sure, for the key was on the outside of it as usual. His repeated knocks produced no answer. Mr Abney was engaged: he was speaking. What! Why did he try to cry out? And why was the cry choked in his throat? Had he, too, seen the mysterious children?

But now everything was quiet, and the door yielded to Stephen's terrified and frantic pushing.